The Diamond
I Wear Is Within

The Diamond I Wear Is Within

Letters of Biblical Encouragement for the Single Woman's Journey

Lynn Gibson

iUniverse, Inc.
New York Lincoln Shanghai

The Diamond I Wear Is Within
Letters of Biblical Encouragement for the Single Woman's Journey

Copyright © 2007 by Lynn Gibson

All rights reserved. No part of this book may be used or reproduced by any means, graphic, electronic, or mechanical, including photocopying, recording, taping or by any information storage retrieval system without the written permission of the publisher except in the case of brief quotations embodied in critical articles and reviews.

iUniverse books may be ordered through booksellers or by contacting:

iUniverse
2021 Pine Lake Road, Suite 100
Lincoln, NE 68512
www.iuniverse.com
1-800-Authors (1-800-288-4677)

ISBN-13:978-0-595-42539-6 (pbk)
ISBN-13: 978-0-595-86868-1 (ebk)
ISBN-10: 0-595-42539-9 (pbk)
ISBN-10: 0-595-86868-1 (ebk)

Printed in the United States of America

The views expressed in this work are solely those of the author and do not necessarily reflect the views of the publisher, and the publisher hereby disclaims any responsibility for them.

Letters in this book are included with the permission of the writers. All the anecdotal illustrations are true and included with the permission of the persons involved. When necessary, certain names have been changed to protect privacy.

All Scripture quotations, unless otherwise indicated, are taken from the *Holy Bible, New International Version*®. NIV®. Copyright © 1973, 1978, 1984 by International Bible Society. Used by permission of Zondervan. All rights reserved. Other versions used include: *THE MESSAGE* (MSG), © Eugene H. Peterson, 1993, 1994, 1995, 1996, 2000, 2001, 2002, used by permission of NavPress Publishing Group; *New American Standard Bible* (NASB), ©1960, 1962, 1963, 1968, 1971, 1972, 1973, 1975, 1977 by The Lockman Foundation, used by permission; and the *Holy Bible, New Living Translation* (NLT), copyright © 1996, used by permission of Tyndale House Publishers, Inc., Wheaton, IL 60189 USA. All rights reserved. Scripture quotations marked (CEV) are from the *Contemporary English Version* © 1991, 1992, 1995 by American Bible Society. Used by Permission.

For:
The 2001 community of "20s" women at
Peninsula Bible Church Cupertino, California.
Thank you for sharing your letters, hearts,
And journeys with me

To Stefani:
Thanks for your authentic faith

To you:
May you find renewal
And refreshment here
"I have you in my heart."—Phil. 1:7a (NASB)

The King's daughter is all glorious within.
—Psalm 45:13a (NASB)

The Stories We Live

A Poem by Stefani Rossi
Littleton, Colorado

Pains of feeling "on the outside" or separated;
Love of independence mixed with a tinge of sorrow over being alone;
Longing to be cherished;
The thrill of being acknowledged;
Struggles to maintain perspective on what is really important.
Epiphanies regarding who we are,
And the longing to become all we could possibly be;
The hope of having all of who we are
Embraced with understanding;
Our pursuits for a sense of belonging—for "home";
This is the stuff of life—the stories we live.

Contents

Acknowledgments xv

Introduction xvii

Chapter 1   When God Passes By 1

Chapter 2   Finding Christ, Following Christ 6

Chapter 3   Waiting for the Lord 11

Chapter 4   The Joy of the Wayfarer 16

Chapter 5   Seeing the Unseen 21

Chapter 6   Love Letter From God 27

Chapter 7   Guard Your Heart 30

Chapter 8   Unveiled and Alluring:
             Some Thoughts on Biblical, Feminine Beauty 35

Chapter 9   Quenching Your Thirst at the River of Life 39

Chapter 10   I Will Change Your Name 44

Chapter 11   You're Invited 49

Chapter 12   Sexual Temptation and the
             Question of Same-sex Love 53

Chapter 13   Eight Words to Change Your Life 60

Chapter 14   Spiritual Slump 65

Chapter 15   Longing for Intimacy 70

Chapter 16   Ten Questions Before Saying "I Do" 74

Chapter 17	Affections of the Heart 81
Chapter 18	Living With Boundaries 84
Chapter 19	Scaling the Depths of Depression 91
Chapter 20	On Being Mentored 96
Chapter 21	The Dance of Life 100
Chapter 22	Hands Open, Palms Up 103
Chapter 23	Contrasting Shadows 109
Chapter 24	Lumpiness of Life 115
Chapter 25	Emerging Identity 119
Chapter 26	Where Do I Belong? 124
Chapter 27	The Diamond I Wear Is Within 133
Chapter 28	Battling Cynicism in a Cynical World 140
Chapter 29	The Stories of Our Lives 146
Chapter 30	Embracing Singleness Amidst the Stings of Life 153

About the Author 161

Notes 163

Acknowledgments

I thank God my Father, and the Lord Jesus Christ, through the indwelling power of the Holy Spirit, for the call, conviction, and completion of this book.

Thank you to the women who have allowed me to reprint your letters and poems and include them in these pages in order to encourage others. You are beautiful writers and authentic wayfarers. You know who you are; you have enriched my life.

Thanks to those of you who have encouraged me with your diamond stories.

Thank you to the many friends who took the time to read the manuscript, in part or full, and provide comment and critique: Michelle Murray, Mary Kay Benz, Harriet Congdon, Anna Bersagel, Lindsay Standish, Lisa Suender, Judy Heaton, Stacy Card, Kim Mewes, John Hanneman, Liz Hanneman, and Brian Morgan.

Thank you to my copyeditor, Jenny Mertes, for polishing the manuscript; to Kim Boston, of BCi Creative, for your innovative cover design; and to Alex Renner, of Pegasus Media Group, for the author photo. Thanks to Terri Nichols for your style and color consulting.

Supreme thanks to my prayer team, including: Michelle, Mary Kay, Cheryl, Heather, Linda, Cary, Nancy, Julie, Lori, Jan, Sheri, and Stefani. Thank you to the prayer groups at The Oaks Classical Christian Academy, and Summit Ridge Christian Fellowship. Thanks to David Wall and Cal Larson for your unwavering enthusiasm. And thanks to my book group gals for your laughter and friendship.

Thank you to Kyle Duncan of Bethany House Publishers, for giving me the initial green light on the concept during a book proposal evaluation.

Thanks to the entire team at iUniverse.

Thank you to my parents and siblings; and my three children, Anna, Peter, and Kate for your continued support through the many seasons of this project.

Finally, thank you to my husband, Jeff, for your loyal love and support in every way possible.

Introduction

Dear Friends:

If you are single, you're in good company. Today, singleness is almost as likely to be an adult's status as marriage. As the twenty-first century unfolds, forty-one percent of all adults have never married or are divorced, widowed, or separated.[1]

Because of this trend, the stigma of singleness is no longer a societal norm, yet the sting often remains. In some corners of Christian culture, single women feel an unspoken pressure to get married and have children, to "*Be intentional about improving your social life,*" or, at the very least, "*Do something!*" A single woman often feels on the "outside" of a church community, or struggles with a vague sense that she is "missing out" on life. Then there is the ticking of the biological clock, which provides internal pressure. How does one "trust God" when the years of child bearing are finite? Though many of these same issues faced single women in past decades, today's cultural landscape is strewn with complexity. The pace of life, overwhelming options, and seeming instability of a constantly changing world can lead single women to self-doubt and disillusionment.

◆ ◆ ◆

If you are single in your 20s and 30s, you most likely have never married and, if you desire marriage, hold onto the hope of meeting someone. Others of you may find yourself suddenly single through divorce or widowhood, perhaps even juggling single parenting. Regardless of your situation, these early adult years will be some of the most tremendous and tumultuous of your life, causing you to confront a multitude of decisions.

For those finishing college there are career questions. Should you choose a job close to your university, return home, or explore the great world beyond? Should you ditch the idea of a "real" job and, instead, travel, do missionary work, or continue your education? There are roommate issues and transitions among your group of friends. You move away from old friends and gain new ones. In whatever place you land, you will seek a community—a similar group of people with shared values—to provide friendship and support. You will look into church groups, clubs, volunteer opportunities, and business networks.

You have left behind the ways of a child and now must face adult considerations. Finances are a never-ending headache as you try to budget and save or just stay ahead of expenses and debt. If you can afford it, you may consider buying a house. You might also ponder the value of an advanced degree. Challenges of self-discipline become central during these years. You will start to develop routines (or at least think about them) regarding exercise and diet, bedtimes and rise times, personal solitude and devotional routines, laundry and "catch up" days.

Your faith must move beyond the faith of your parents, or the faith of your college years—perhaps carried along by the inertia of abundant opportunities for religious activity—to a personal faith. You are now on your own, which means you can choose to attend church, or not. You can choose to walk with God, or not.

◆ ◆ ◆

If you are single in your 40s and 50s, and have never married, you are probably frustrated with the dating scene. You may be wrestling with the question: Why are some men so seemingly afraid to commit? The structures of your life are stable, but (you wonder) perhaps *too stable*. You have a home, steady employment, and friendships, though sometimes wonder, Does God still see me? Does he really care about the desires of my heart? Am I missing anything he has for me? As God's daughter, you want to be realistic about preparing for your future, while not growing cynical or resigned. There is the delicate balance between operating with a sense of independence that has been fine-tuned over the years, while still keeping your heart open, tender, and available for new relationships and God's gentle sculpting of your character.

You may be single because of divorce or widowhood. Such life changes bring fear and insecurity. You may wonder: Can I handle being alone financially and emotionally? Will I make poor decisions on my own? Will I get involved with someone who is wrong for me simply because I'm so very lonely?

◆ ◆ ◆

If you are single in your 60s and beyond, you may struggle with loneliness, helplessness, and the questions, Does anyone need me? Am I relevant? You are adjusting to handling decisions alone, whether tax preparation or car maintenance. While a degree of uncertainty fills these days, there are also opportunities to explore new places, pursue burgeoning passions, and discover how God might be clarifying your calling.

◆ ◆ ◆

One area of restlessness among single women of all stages is the heart and its longings. Taking notice of an interesting man begins a rollercoaster of emotions; dating him can be complicated; and breaking up often leads to heartache. Relationships with men are like a dance where very seldom does it appear we get in step. Most of the time it feels like each is stepping on the other's toes. Yet, because God created us to be male and female, we still determine the dance is worth the discomfort.

On the days when you are feeling content with this season of your life, you may find yourself broadsided by the misguided though well-intentioned reminders from married women that you are *still single*, as if you needed to be told. You attend yet another wedding and it is not your own. "When are you going to get married?" an older woman asks, as if you could predict the day. A hundred years ago, chances are that you could have predicted your wedding day. At the beginning of the twentieth century, the majority of the American adult population was married. Today, the average age for first marriages among women in the United States is twenty-seven. That is as high as it has ever been.[2]

For those without faith, the journey of singleness can be murky and unsettling. One secular author writes, "There is the sense of overwhelming change and that the roadmap has disappeared."[3] That may be true for those who don't have a Guide, yet for those who have believed in Jesus Christ and are saved, the roadmap is certain and firmly established. Jesus says, "I am the way and the truth and the life."[4]

Hebrews 13:8 reminds us that, "Jesus Christ is the same yesterday and today and forever." In the middle of the uncertainties of single life is a living, personal God who longs to know you and be known by you. Your roadmap is the truth of Scripture. These words of life flow from the living God through the personal love letter he has written you in the Bible. He has much to tell you. He wants to guide your path. He wants to be your first and greatest love.

If you are willing, God wants to transform you into the glorious image of his Son, Jesus. He wants you to shine as a single woman in a despairing world. You may not be wearing a diamond on your finger, but the diamond you wear is within as you reflect the radiance of Christ by surrendering to his transforming power in your life. This is how the Apostle Paul describes your shimmering self in 2 Corinthians 3:18:

> And we, who with unveiled faces all reflect the Lord's glory, are being transformed into his likeness with ever-increasing glory, which comes from the Lord, who is the Spirit.

In the following pages, my intention is to shine a light on this Transformer of Lives, the Guide who will teach you and set you free to live with dazzling beauty during this, and all seasons of life. The Lord has called me to a very specific goal in these writings, to encourage and equip, remind and refresh you of biblical truth.[5]

Over the years, I have received numerous letters from single women. They are beautifully written, heartfelt snapshots of the highs and lows, the triumphs and heartbreaks of their lives. With their permission, while maintaining their anonymity, I include many of their letters and poems here, along with my letters of response on various topics. Some of the letters I address outright. Others are included as a "jumping off" point from which I explore a particular issue. These conversational musings are as varied as the women themselves. Here is a sampling of some of the women's lives represented through these letters (with names changed). Perhaps they are your stories as well:

- Cary is learning what it means to respect Matt and communicate with him.
- Becky feels like life is passing her by.
- Melissa continues to struggle with deep loneliness and depression.
- Lisa is adjusting to her boyfriend living nearby. She desires more community in her living situation.
- Stephanie bought a house with her parents and is adjusting to maintaining her own identity while living in community with them.
- Kristi has been sick off and on for the last few months. She is dating Jason and enjoying their time together.
- Pam just moved to a new city and a new job and is struggling to fit in both places.
- Donna has gained two new roommates and is adjusting accordingly.
- Linda is struggling with same-sex love and drug addiction.
- Nicole is looking for a job and trying to make ends meet.
- Kim is having a hard time with housemates. Her dad has been deployed with the military and she deals with fear.

She is excited about a bonus at work that enabled her to buy a new car.
- Erin is facing the possibility of surgery and wonders if she should move back home with her parents.
- Anna is in a long-term relationship with Scott and wonders about marriage. They are struggling with sexual boundaries.
- Amy feels like she is slacking spiritually.
- Christy is recovering from her failed marriage while trying to raise a preschooler.
- Michelle struggles with the shame of "not having it all together." She is afraid people judge her because of her rough edges.
- Laurie is starting her first year of full-time teaching and is exhausted.
- Lauren moved to the city and recently started a new job.
- Jan is reeling from the sudden, tragic death of her husband.
- Kathryn has been recently hurt by her best friend and is trying to figure out what it means to love in the midst of it.
- Cindy is finding it hard to balance work, ministry, friends, and personal time.
- Rebecca just ended a long-term relationship and is nursing a broken heart.

These are among the themes I address in the pages ahead. Each chapter begins with a letter from a single woman, followed with my letter of response on a particular topic, and ending with a "postscript to ponder," a devotional thought for your consideration. This book is not meant to be a counseling tome or even an advice column, but rather some small servings of what I pray is God's wisdom from the vantage point of a friend and fellow sojourner who cares very much about your well-being and the choices you are making. I hope through these letters to turn your focus toward God, the one who loves you and is writing a poem of your life. I have you in my heart.

Chapter 1

Dear Lynn:

My week has been full of divine appointments. On Tuesday night, I was on my way home when I looked to my left and noticed a woman struggling to walk through the snow and trying to hitch a ride.

I was in the center lane and couldn't pull over, so I just stopped my car and put on my hazard lights. She made it to my car without being smashed. Her speech was a little slurred, and so internally, I started making all sorts of evaluations, and I'm not proud of that. She asked if I would give her a couple bucks for smokes, and I said no, but asked instead if she needed food. So, we went grocery shopping, and she was amazed to the point of being uncomfortable. As we talked, she said something about me being spiritual, and I said yes, to which she replied, "I don't know what you believe, but I'm a Christian myself." She hadn't been to church in a while, but said she'd like to come with me. We are to show no partiality, right?

I am humbled that as I tried to make it home through snow, Jesus showed up in the face of this woman who was in need, and he gave me the gift of meeting her need in a small way.

I am pressed on to wonder what miracles I would see on a daily basis if only I would drop my guard more often; the same guard that whispers to me to stay with my own kind, remain with the people who understand me, abide in safety, pass by the people with obvious aching need, and hang on to the snap judgments I make, based on initial impressions.

I am pressed on with the uncomfortable reality of what it means to practice showing no partiality, practice being a neighbor, practice hospitality to a stranger, and to become obedient to the whispers of God.

When God Passes By

We have seen his glory, the glory of the One and Only.
—John 1:14b

We have to learn to live in the grey day according to what we saw on the mount.—Oswald Chambers

At dawn I saw Carmel rising from the sea into a blazing sky of deep blue shot through with red. The beauty of the landscape hit me with almost physical violence.—Elie Wiesel

Dear Friends,

As a senior in high school, I ran cross-country. I had no natural talent for the sport, but I had washed out of gymnastics a year earlier and was looking to be part of a girls' sports team. When my friends joined cross-country, I also signed up and soon found myself running sprints up the hills around our school. My coach assigned me to what he determined was the least competitive cross-country event: the two-mile race. I had never run two miles in my life, yet as the training got underway I realized that I could condition my body to go the distance. Then came the first track meet. I wasn't concerned about coming in last place; my goal was simply to finish the race. What I didn't count on was being lapped—numerous times. I ran so slowly in my progression to complete eight laps around the track that nearly all of the other runners overtook and passed me, not once but by two laps or more. The race was passing me by. I felt defeated.

A friend in her early thirties recently shared with me her innermost cry: "I feel like life is passing me by." I understood her heart as I recalled those memories of being lapped in cross-country so long ago. My friend wants to be married. She longs to be loved by a man. She desires to have children. She wishes to be in a satisfying career. She hopes to have some promise of a permanent address. She dreams of financial security. She would like a clear sense of calling. Yet, for now, the details of her life are murky. She looks around at others who have seemingly "arrived" in lives of relative certainty, and she is distraught. While so many others are "getting on with their lives," my friend feels left behind. Life, she says, is passing her by.

I wonder if Moses felt that way as he tended sheep in the empty and vast desert of Midian. He had lots of time to reflect on the strange detour his life had taken. Once an Egyptian prince, Moses had been trained in the Egyptian military, enjoyed the luxuries of palace living, and could count on a future laden with power, wealth, and influence. Now he was a stranger in a strange land, married to a foreigner, and performing the job of shepherd—a job he had been raised to detest. That was the scene as Moses wandered up Mt. Horeb, the mountain of God, and came upon a bush that was burning, yet not consumed. The God of Abraham, Isaac, and Jacob appeared to Moses through this burning bush, calling Moses to lead the Israelites out of Egypt. Because of the Exodus, Moses experienced God in a tangible and intimate way, which led to his bold invitation in Exodus 33: "Now show me your glory."

In an amazing dialogue, the Lord replied, "When my glory passes by, I will put you in a cleft in the rock and cover you with my hand until I have passed by."[1] This was a defining moment in Moses' faith walk when the Lord provided a striking, visible manifestation of his Deity.

"I will cause all my *goodness* to pass in front of you," the Lord told Moses. God could have chosen to make manifest to Moses any one of his invisible attributes. He could have said, "I will cause my *power* to pass in front of you," or sovereignty, majesty, or splendor. Yet, he chose to display his goodness, a word that means "that which is pleasing, beneficial, and intrinsically good." And so the Lord passed by. From the cleft of a rock, Moses beheld God's glory—not even his *full* glory, just a shadow of his glory—and it was enough.

It can be the same for you. For those the Lord knows by name, he wants to provide you a taste of his goodness that flows from his unfailing love. "Taste and see that the Lord is good," the psalmist writes.[2] During moments when I have needed it most, the Lord has passed by me and shown me his goodness in some memorable ways. Once, I was driving to the airport after a long week of parenting three small children while my husband was on a business trip. I was exhausted. As my car rounded the hill and dropped down into the valley, there was a blazing sunset in brilliant colors of red and orange. I felt the Lord's goodness flow over me in such a profound way that I had to pull over and stop the car. Other times, God's goodness has come by way of the Holy Spirit directing me to a verse of Scripture perfectly suited to the need of the moment; or by a word of encouragement from a friend that refocused my gaze on God. Once, when my husband was experiencing a possible layoff at work and I was fearful of the future, I drove by an empty field of weeds. There, by the sidewalk, a small bird was gathering bits of straw and debris to make a nest. God's voice came immediately and profoundly into my heart: "I am Jehovah Jireh, the God who provides. Trust me to provide for you."

For a reminder of God's goodness, let us, like Moses, boldly ask God, "Show me your glory." First, though, let us make sure that we have not wandered into a place where sin has blocked us from beholding his glory. Let us examine our hearts and repent of any known area where we have "missed the mark," sin's definition, and see to it that we are living in accordance with God's Word. Then, let us watch and wait for the Lord to pass by in a memorable display of his goodness. When that happens, your heart will be stirred to worship. The certainty of God's goodness toward you will replace your concerns that life is passing you by. God is not withholding any good thing from you as a single woman. Do you believe that?

The Lord loves to stir our senses with his presence; to awaken elation through his beauty. Yet we cannot live for the glimpses; we live by faith in the person of Jesus. If you want to see God's glory on a daily basis, then gaze upon Jesus, "the radiance of God's glory and the exact representation of his being."[3] Jesus says, "He who beholds me beholds the One who sent me." Jesus prays a beautiful prayer on our behalf: "Father,

I want these whom you've given me *to be with me*, so they can see my glory. You gave me the glory because you loved me even before the world began."[4]

Through this season of singleness, Jesus desires that you choose to be with him so he can fill your days with himself and the security that comes from the knowledge of his lavish love toward you. If you are walking with Jesus daily, be encouraged that you are on track with God's design for your life. Rather than choosing to be mired in the notion that *life is passing you by*, consider that God is waiting to *pass by you*, to offer you reminders of his goodness through his glorious Son, Jesus.

"The Lord is good to those whose hope is in him, to the one who seeks him."[5] Do you trust in God's goodness toward you? Do you believe that God's heart is for you? Settle that once and for all. Then ask God, "Show me your glory!" as you fix your gaze upon Jesus. He awaits your invitation and longs to hear you say what the psalmist declared in Psalm 27:13, "I am still confident of this: I will see the goodness of the Lord in the land of the living."

I have you in my heart.

Postscript to ponder: How has God passed by you, giving you a glimpse of his glory? What might he be trying to whisper to you right now?

Chapter 2

Dear Lynn:

I tried to catch you last weekend on Sunday afternoon but, alas, no success. So, I figured I'd catch you up by e-mail and ask you the question I've been wondering about since last Sunday.

Thank you for introducing me to Jesus Christ through the Alpha course. Now that I'm a Christian, what do I do?

Finding Christ, Following Christ

But seek first his kingdom and his righteousness, and all these things will be given to you as well.—Matthew 6:33

Dear Friends:

If you are seeking Christ or are a new follower of Christ, perhaps you would benefit from reading a letter I wrote to Marcie, my friend who recently said a simple prayer of faith. Her prayer acknowledged that Jesus Christ is the Son of God, admitted her sin and need for forgiveness, and accepted God's gift of salvation and new life. This letter is for her, and for you, whether you are considering a relationship with God through Jesus Christ, or are wondering what to do with your new Christian faith.

Dear Marcie,

In the presence of some friends this week, you said a prayer that will change the course of your life, both on earth and in heaven. Jesus came to dwell with you that day and will never leave you. The prayer you prayed is often called *The Sinner's Prayer*, because in it you admitted that you are a sinner. Sin is not only doing wrong things, it is being wrongly related to God. Sin is the inclination to live apart from God, deliberately and emphatically choosing to live independent of him.[1] The truth is, we can't live apart from God for very long and have it go well with us, truly well, for the long term. We are broken and rebellious people who are stuck in a pit. We need a rescuer. You had the humility to cry out to God and accept his rescue. In your prayer, you essentially said: Help me God! I'm stuck in this pit. Forgive me for the sin of thinking I could run my life independently of you. I willingly choose today to lay down my rebellion and accept your plan of rescue, which is the cross of Jesus, the Son of God, who is my Redeemer.

At that moment, God forgave you and granted you eternal life.[2] On that day, you began a new relationship with a God who exists in three persons: Father, Son, and Spirit. Like any relationship, to know someone and grow to love and trust him takes time. The more time you spend investing in getting to know God through Jesus, the closer you will become to him and the more you will benefit from this relationship. That is why I call the Christian life a *faith journey*. By faith, you are walking through life with the God of the Universe and, over time, he will teach you and you will find that he is changing you through a process called spiritual maturity. This journey will not always be easy, nor will it be trouble free. God's goal for you is not that you experience a life of ease, but something far more satisfying—a life brimming with more and more of himself.

Now that you are a Christian, you must nourish your faith. Each day, I would encourage you to do whatever it takes to deliberately remind yourself of what you believe, in order to train yourself in the habit of faith. Some faith *ingredients* are necessary to grow in Christ. Without these things, you will become dry and wilt, or become stagnant. A flower planted in the ground needs several things to grow: roots, water, sunshine, air, and nutrients. It is the same for you, as a follower of Christ. Please indulge me as I use the analogy of gardening to explain your faith journey with Christ.

First, you will need deep roots as the foundation of your faith so you will grow strong.

Deep roots come from studying God's Word, the Bible, as the firm foundation of your faith. I highly encourage you to join a group Bible study and begin to learn how to dig into God's Word with other Christians. I also encourage you to read the Bible on your own, taking notes on what you discover and writing down your questions.

Water comes in the form of worship, which will refresh you. God created us to worship. The word *worship* is the idea of kissing God's face in an expression of reverence and devotion. You can worship God through singing and silence, prayer and poetry, studying and serving. Your understanding of worship will be enlarged as you proceed on your faith journey. As you grow to love God, you will naturally want to worship him.

Sunshine is an awareness of God's presence in your life each day, a light that penetrates the darkness. Always try to be aware that he is present. As Brother Lawrence writes, "Practice the presence of God." Look for his movements and acknowledge his workings. Talk to him and spend quiet moments listening.

Air is the infiltrating work of the Holy Spirit who will teach you, comfort you, and guide you. The idea of the Holy Spirit is a difficult one to grasp. Anything of the supernatural realm is mysterious and complex for we who live in the physical world, but over time, you will come to appreciate the Spirit's whisperings in your heart.

Finally, you need *nutrients*, spiritual encouragement provided to you by the company of other Christians. The Bible refers to this as *fellowship* or *community*.[3] In order to grow in faith, Christians need each other. This is why it is important to find a church and attend it regularly. God doesn't need our church attendance; we do.

Those are the necessary elements of your spiritual sojourn with God: Bible study, worship, prayer, an awareness of God's presence, an ear attuned to the Holy Spirit, and community with other followers of Christ. Establishing these components in your life takes work, discipline, and sacrifice, though it is a worthy process since the investment will provide you the greatest friendship of your life, not to mention unimaginable adventures. Let the journey begin.

I have you in my heart.

Postscript to ponder: Which of these essential ingredients for a life of spiritual growth is lacking in your life, and how might you cultivate it?

Chapter 3

Dear Lynn:

I just got home from my 20s group. It was a good night of worship, study, and fellowship. As I sat in the host's family room surrounded by my peers, my friends, my kindred spirits, I quickly became very aware of the pain that existed in their hearts. One struggles with her health, another with her deep sense of loneliness. A housemate of mine struggles with a broken relationship, another has her uncertainty about the future, and my closest friend feels completely inadequate. And there is my own pain of lost relationships.

The pain runs deep for so many. I didn't know what to do, so I did all I could do. I praised my God in heaven, clinging to his promise to use the pain *for our good and his glory* this side of heaven, and to wipe it away on the other side.

Waiting. That is what lingers in my heart. We wait; wait for understanding, wait for his strength, wait for his return. Pain exists, sometimes as a result of sin, sometimes as a result of life. We can't maneuver our lives. Life is not a chess game.

We need to rest; we need to wait. The hope comes from knowing that God will use it all regardless of the source. God has impressed it on my heart to tell you all this. I hope it gives you a sense of the place some of us are in.

Waiting for the Lord
(While Tending a Broken Heart)

I would have despaired unless I had believed that I would see the goodness of the Lord in the land of the living. Wait for the Lord; Be strong, and let your heart take courage; Yes, wait for the Lord.—Psalm 27:13 (NASB)

Dear Friends:

My friend's heart has been broken to pieces. It feels shattered beyond repair. She has been dating a guy for a year—a great guy—and he led her to believe they were progressing toward engagement and marriage. Then, without warning, he broke up with her, without any discussion. The reasons seem woefully inadequate. He has disappeared from her life, and she is devastated. She is trying to pick up the fragments of her heart, but her pain is unbearable.

We live in a broken world filled with heartache wherever we turn. As followers of Jesus Christ, we are not exempt from afflictions. They seem to come to us as surely as the morning. Some of the pain we experience is our own doing, from choices we have made presently or in the past. Other times, our pain is the result of a fallen world filled with selfishness, strife, and sin. Often, as in my friend's case, pain comes to us by those who sting us with their hurtful ways, whether intentional or not. Regardless of its origin, pain can overwhelm and threaten to swallow us whole. What are we to do? Our culture counsels us to carefully manage pain through medication, avoidance, or blame. Or, create a diversion to redirect our focus: A new hobby! A new wardrobe! Botox! Build a wall of cynicism around your heart, or dull your senses through spending, addictions, or gratification, so you will never risk feeling such pain again.

King David, a man after God's own heart, took a different approach. In Psalm 42, he pours out a lament of his physical agony, emotional turmoil, faltering faith, and spiritual discouragement. In this outpouring of tears, he cries out to an audience of one, the living God. "My tears have been my food day and night," David writes, "while men say to me all day long, 'Where is your God?' I say to God my Rock, 'Why have you forgotten me? Why must I go about mourning?'"[1] David confronts his pain; moreover, *he embraces it* through written expression. In total honesty, he tells God his heart: This is how I feel. This is what I need. Where are you? Why does it seem that you are distant? As David gives voice to the ache of his soul, a curious thing happens. The ache becomes a gateway, an entrance into the presence of God himself.[2] "Deep calls to deep in the roar of your waterfalls; all your waves and breakers have swept over me. By day the Lord directs his love, at night his song is with me—a prayer to the God of my life."[3]

As David walks into his pain, describing its force through the avenue of poetry, the Lord meets him on the pathway of agony and begins to lift him out of its depths. In Psalm 34, David writes, "The Lord is close to the brokenhearted and saves those who are crushed in spirit." Through his journey into grief, David experiences God in a new way. "Taste and see that the Lord is good," he writes. Nothing of his circumstances is good, but David recognizes that by embracing the pain, the Lord uses it to direct David into his presence, a place of refuge.

There are two more commands that David exhorts the downcast soul to follow, found in Psalm 42:11:

> Why are you downcast, O my soul? Why so disturbed within me? Put your hope in God, for I will yet (still) praise him, my Savior and my God.

First, David suggests that we put our hope in God. Hope is one of those life-sustaining words found more often in the Bible than in our cultural vernacular. Hope is a confident expectation that God is who he says he is, and will do what he says he will do. Our hearts were created to hope, but when they get broken, hope gets heaved to the sidelines. In its place, cynicism takes up residence as our constant companion. David exhorts us to give cynicism the boot and reclaim hope, placing it firmly in God's unchanging character. The Lord is trustworthy, faithful, and lavishly loving. He will not disappoint.

After hope has been reestablished, David exhibits a behavior that seems counter to the broken heart: he offers praise. "I will still praise him, my Savior and my God," he writes.

Praise is not the first thing I think of when my heart has been crushed. I would rather cry, wallow, despair, escape, or take revenge. In all these behaviors, the focus is on me. When uttering praise to God, the focus is on him. Praise is an expression of gratitude and devotion to God. Praise means to enumerate, or list, the attributes of God, to acknowledge his perfections, works, and benefits. When our reservoirs are depleted, praise becomes a choice of the *will* not of our *feelings*, which is why the Bible often refers to a "sacrifice of praise." Praise is the act of sacrificially laying down my Self's dashed glory on the altar and focusing, instead, on God's glory. "Praise and worship" are often mentioned together in Scripture because once we enumerate God's attributes—majesty, sovereignty, faithfulness, holiness, truth, grace, and so on—our natural response is worship, a word encompassing the idea of devotion and reverence to God. David suggests that we hope and praise even while our soul is downcast. This requires a choice to will and to act, regardless of the state of our feelings. By doing so, God will meet you in your pain and begin to lift you from its depths.

Friends, if you suffer from a broken heart, I encourage you to choose the way of King David rather than the counsel of the world. Embrace the ache and give it a voice through poetry or journaling. Don't worry that you're not a writer. Grab a pen and plumb pain's depths, writing a lament to God. Leave nothing out and make it an honest cry of your heart. Consciously show cynicism the door and usher in hope. Spend time regularly praising God, as an act of sacrificial worship, even if you don't feel like it. Then wait for God. Watch how he can turn the ache into a gateway into his presence. Let your senses, weary as they are, become aware of God. Perhaps a sunset is his reminder of faithfulness to you; perhaps a song is his personal lullaby to you; perhaps a scent in the air whispers his promise to return fragrance to your life; or a butterfly becomes a sign of his certain transformation of your heart. Watch him use various pictures in the physical realm to express his heart for you, and his love for you beyond the measure of earth and sky.

Finally, take courage. You will see the goodness of the Lord in the land of the living. Why? Because God does not withhold good from those he loves, from those who walk uprightly.[4] Pain was never part of God's perfect plan, but restoration is. Does God relish inflicting pain on his children? Not at all! Rather, God uses pain (the result of a fallen world) to reveal himself, to give us a taste of transcendence, and to enlarge our hearts so we can experience his love more fully. Will my friend ever love again? Yes, and it will be in a way that is fuller than ever. That is God's business, to bring about healing and restoration.

Jesus grieves your broken heart. He longs to be your comfort. He desires that you would let him gather you to himself and embrace you in the shadow of his wings. He will direct his love toward you if you will let him. Don't escape, don't hide, don't turn bitter, and don't diminish your pain. When the pain seems unbearable, don't bear it. Give it to Jesus and wait to see his goodness lavished upon you.

> Let us settle it forever and forever that God is love, and that everything he does or permits, he does in love. When anything sad or painful comes, seek to find his presence in it, and to get a loving view of him first of all, so that we can see in the very beginning of everything, painful or sorrowful, my Heavenly Father is in this thing. His presence envelops it and he is love. When the outcome of it is made visible, I shall see that it was for my good and his glory.—J.W. Watson

I have you in my heart.

Postscript to ponder: Are you in pain? If so, embrace it, ask God to meet you in the midst of it, and allow him to lift you from its depths.

Chapter 4

Dear Lynn:

The road to nowhere had a small, life-changing detour on it. I did not expect to make friends who would truly be called friends. My life, though lived in a world of chaos, was safe. I knew everyone, and everyone knew me.

In my past, the paths and roads went everywhere leading nowhere. Reality wasn't real, and love never truly existed—just false hopes, lies, and promises that fall through holes.

Then a hand reaches through the clouds, plucks me off the road, and plops me on a well-lighted path.

The sun has not yet risen today, and it is almost seven o'clock. I did get to see the sliver of the crescent moon though, and that held just as much beauty as the rising sun. Have a beautiful day.

The Joy of the Wayfarer

> Let us sing alleluia here on earth, while we still live in anxiety so that we may sing it one day in heaven in full security. God's praises are sung both there and here. But here they are sung in anxiety, there in security; here they are sung by those destined to die, there by those destined to live forever; here they are sung in hope, there in hope's fulfillment; here they are sung by wayfarers, there by those living in their own country. So then, let us sing now, not in order to enjoy a life of leisure, but in order to lighten our labors. You should sing as wayfarers do—sing, but continue your journey—sing then, but keep going.—St. Augustine

Dear Friends:

"Sing as wayfarers do...." These words stir my heart. They help me envision an eternal home I have not yet seen. They bestow upon me courage and hope. In short, Augustine's words bring great joy.

Joy. This small word packs immense meaning. From the Latin word *gaudium*, joy (and its synonym sisters: mirth, gladness, delight, and rejoice) is found hundreds of times in the Bible. Though the journey is hard, there is much joy to be found among followers of Jesus. When I asked a group of my friends, "What brings you joy?" their answers gushed forth from exuberant hearts: friends, family, spring, siblings, flowers, chocolate, puppies, lazy days, candlelight, a chick flick, rainfall, a good night's sleep, a vanilla latté, a revitalizing run, a riveting book.

If it is true, as C. S. Lewis once wrote, that "joy is the serious business of heaven," then perhaps we, as citizens of that faraway country, should take a moment to study this shrouded mystery called joy.

The Bible says we can express joy with our whole disposition. We can be joyful with our heart, our soul, and even our eyes. In various passages, Scripture shows us that one can find joy through gaining wisdom, sharing a kind word, meditating on God's law, increasing in righteousness, and loving one another. It cites passages where men and women in biblical times experienced joy at weddings, feasts, celebrations, coronations, and battle victories. But all these joyous occasions pale in comparison to the most frequently cited reason for joy in Scripture: *the Lord and his salvation.* Psalm 35:9 (NASB) says, "And my soul shall rejoice in the Lord; It shall *exult* [exceedingly leap for joy] in His salvation."

The mystery of biblical joy is that it is rooted in a *Person*, the Lord Jesus Christ, whereas secular joy (what I would call happiness) is rooted in *pleasure.* Because the secular world does not know the Person, it cannot know biblical joy, but only fleeting happiness, based on the temporal gratification of a desire. The world focuses on the *object* that brings happiness—the gift rather than the Giver. Followers of Jesus understand that all gifts we have to enjoy point to the Giver of gifts, God, who offered us the greatest gift of all in his Son.

Jesus knew the secret to cultivating biblical joy. In one of his last teachings, he unveils the mystery of joy in John 15, saying:

> I am the vine, you are the branches; he who abides in me, and I in him, he bears much fruit, for apart from me you can do nothing. If you keep my commandments, you will abide in my love, just as I have kept my Father's commandments and abide in his love. These things I have spoken to you so *that my joy may be in you,* and *that your joy may be made full.*[1]

Joy matters to Jesus: his joy in us, our joy made full. Joy is the natural outcome of a life rightly related to God through faith in Christ. Jesus says, "Abide in me," using the analogy of a branch that must derive its source of life from the vine. *Abide* means to remain, and if we remain in Jesus—deriving all our life from him—the natural outpouring will be what the Bible calls the Fruit of the Spirit, found in Galatians 5:22. In this profound list of "fruit," the first is love and the second is joy. In order to produce such fruit, we must abide in Jesus as the source of all life.

So how do we derive life from Jesus? By spending time with him, by reading his Word and keeping his commandments, by talking and listening to him, and by surrendering our agendas and priorities to him. When you continue doing these things day in and day out for the rest of your days, you will discover another mystery of joy. You will begin to understand that joy can also be found in the midst of suffering. Because biblical joy is rooted in the person of Jesus, sorrow enlarges the Christian's capacity for joy. Jesus alludes to this mystery when he says, "Therefore you too have grief now; but I will see you again, and your heart will rejoice, and no one will take your joy away from you."[2]

The Apostle Paul well understood the intermixing of suffering and joy. In Romans 5:3–5 (NASB), Paul exhorts us to, "exult in our tribulations [troubles]." He explains that tribulation brings about perseverance, proven character, and hope. James, too, understood this mysterious mingling of joy and affliction. He writes, "Consider it pure joy, my brothers, whenever you face trials of many kinds, because you know that the testing of your faith develops perseverance. Perseverance must finish its work so that you may be mature and complete, not lacking anything."[3]

On our own strength, we cannot fabricate joy in the midst of suffering. Such self-effort produces only a disingenuous facade. But, if we abide in Jesus, remaining close to the source of life, we will discover that, amazingly, our identity is so rooted in Christ that we fix our gaze not on our difficult circumstance, but on future glory. "For our light and momentary troubles are achieving for us an eternal glory that far outweighs them all. So we fix our eyes not on what is seen, but on what is unseen. For what is seen is temporary, but what is unseen is eternal."[4]

Joy is the result of a transformed perspective that enables the wayfarer to keep singing. Continue to enjoy all God has given you that is joyous while deeply rooting yourself in Christ for the inevitable day when sorrow will come. You will discover that with sorrow is an accompanying joy: not happiness but, instead, the deep-seated capacity to rejoice in the person of Jesus.

"If God has made your cup sweet, drink it with grace; if he has made it bitter, drink it in communion with him," writes Oswald Chambers. "Be rightly related to God, find your joy there, and out of you will flow rivers of living water."[5]

I have you in my heart.

Postscript to ponder: Are you deriving life from any source apart from Jesus? Could this other source be stealing your joy?

Chapter 5

Dear Lynn:

The year was good for me. I spent four weeks working in Southern California and enjoyed every moment of it. I still marvel at the way my work makes my soul sing. I have heard people say that true worship is doing what God created you to do. In fact, if my memory serves me correctly, during a study in the book of Genesis, I learned that the Hebrew word for work and worship is the same word.

In Southern California, I experienced this mystery of work being worship. It was a heavenly experience, and my attempts to articulate it through words do not do it justice. As I write these words, I long to see my Savior face to face and understand the mystery fully.

Seeing the Unseen

> He has made everything beautiful in its time. He has also set eternity in the hearts of men; yet they cannot fathom what God has done from beginning to end.—Ecclesiastes 3:11

Dear Friends:

My friend Pat calls them God sightings. I call them glimpses of eternity. They surprise me when I am least expecting them. When I catch even a shadow of this unseen realm, it silences me. It stirs me to renewed hope and enlarges my longing for God. Yet, not everyone "sees the unseen." The Bible says that such a glimpse belongs to those who have eyes and ears attuned to the quiet whisperings of God and the invisible epic story he is telling.

Elisha had an unforgettable God sighting. Called "the man of God" in Second Kings 6, Elisha was a prophet serving the king of Israel. It so happened that the king of Aram was at war with Israel, yet he knew he didn't stand a chance against God's people. Each time he moved his men to advance upon Israel, Elisha would prophesy their whereabouts, and the Israelite army would meet them in battle. Not surprisingly, the king of Aram became enraged. "Go, find out where Elisha is, so I can send men and capture him," the king ordered. The report came back: "He is in Dothan." The king of Aram sent horses, chariots, and a strong force to Dothan. They went by night and surrounded the city.

When Elisha's servant went out early the next morning, he saw the enemy had surrounded the city. "Oh, my lord, what shall we do?" he asked Elisha. "Don't be afraid," the prophet replied. "Those who are with us are greater than those who are with them." Then Elisha prayed, "O Lord, open my servant's eyes so he may see." The Lord answered Elisha's prayer and opened the servant's eyes so that he saw what Elisha was already seeing: the hillsides full of God's heavenly army of horses and chariots, surrounding and protecting Elisha! Elisha's eyes stayed fixed on the unseen realm of God's sovereign might, and he was filled with courage.

◆   ◆   ◆

Eyes fixed on the unseen. For the woman whose goal is to walk by faith as a follower of Christ, this is a great mystery: to eat, sleep, drive, work, play, and live in the physical world while keeping an eye and ear and heart attuned to the transcendent, spiritual realm where God dwells and moves among us. God doesn't dismiss the physical world: this is where he has placed us. Rather, he uses the physical realm where we live to accomplish his spiritual purposes in us and through us. Putting on eternal eyes, then, means to discover God's fingerprints in our lives. These are the "ah-hah" moments when the Holy Spirit figuratively pulls back the curtain of our circumstances and lets us "see" God's hand working invisibly through our jobs, conversations, classes, ministries, and moments of quiet to reveal his character and bring us into deeper communion with him.

One friend I know is reeling from a heartbreaking loss. After a year of loving a man who had communicated his intentions to marry her, he suddenly broke up with her. She loves God but her heart is so hurt she can hardly bear the pain. How will God use this ache to accomplish his purposes? What is he doing that is beyond what our eyes can see?

Two of my friends were physically abused as young girls by men they most trusted. How can God bring any good out of this to further his kingdom, and how will he accomplish his promise to restore them?

Having eternal eyes means looking beyond the here and now—what we see happening to us—and setting our vision on the invisible, faithful God who "... causes all things to work together for good to those who love God, to those who are called according to His purpose."[1] Seeing the unseen means watching, waiting, and trusting God to use your brokenness, car accident, promotion, friendship, hardship, frustration, financial shortcoming, accomplishment, demotion, housing situation, misunderstanding, death of a loved one—you fill in the blank—to tell his grand story of love and redemption.

Several years ago, I was sitting in a quiet chapel on the campus of Princeton University waiting for a memorial service to start. To even be there with eight close high school friends was surreal. We had traveled more than a thousand miles to grieve the unfathomable and abrupt death of a dear friend we had known since junior high who had died in a car accident just weeks earlier. He hadn't even turned forty. I was very much in the physical world as I sat in that hushed chapel. I noticed the pale yellow walls and glossy white trim. The pipe organ was majestic, and the squeaky wooden pews hinted at stories centuries old. It was raining outside—God's tears—and during the first eulogy, a loud thunderclap struck as if heaven itself was announcing its presence. Time stood still and, without warning, my friends and I were ushered in our spirits to another place, to glimpse the unseen realm. Our tears took us from the end of ourselves into a spiritual dimension where God was palpably present and angels (while unseen) seemed to be ministering to us. The heavenly veil was pulled back long enough for us to taste and see that the Lord is divinely good. It was a sweet moment in the midst of heartbreaking agony over the reality of death. Our communal ache became a gateway for the Lord to usher us into his heavenly throne room (though seen through a mirror dimly) where we, even in our human state, were given a brushing with the glory, holiness, and exuberant joy of eternity. Never have I experienced the melding of both realms, the seen and unseen, as I did at that moment. Earthly pain and eternal exuberance separated by a thin veil. Present grieving mixed with heavenly peace. Myriad troubling questions, yet a settled assurance. In my heart, I heard the message, *"Wait. This is not the end of the story. The end is coming and it is good."*

Out of God's goodness, he allows his children to see beyond the mundane to the majestic; to glimpse his wonder amidst the wearisome; to feel his touch as we toil. Why does God give us such glimpses? Like Elisha, maybe it is to give us courage; like the Apostle Paul on the road to Damascus, maybe it is to cause us to stop and turn from our agenda to his. Like Isaiah, maybe it is to instruct us in a specific calling. Or, like Moses at the burning bush, maybe it is to initiate intimacy with us and show us his glory. God is mystery and his reasons are mysterious, but I don't want to miss a single glimpse he has in store for me.

Of course, we can't live for the glimpses: we live by faith. The disciple should not live for the tastes of eternity: we live to obey, serve, pray, worship, and press on to maturity. When God is silent toward us, we need to keep walking by faith. When he speaks, we are grateful. The command of Second Corinthians 4:18 is to "fix our eyes on what is unseen." This means we need to divert our attention away from the physical world and its fixation on celebrity, materialism, gratification, pleasure, and perversions and, instead, fix, or *glue our gaze*, on the eternal. What should we gaze upon as part of the unseen realm? Here are a few mysteries I've determined to ponder: the person of Jesus and his command to "abide in me and I in you"; the transforming power of the Holy Spirit; the awesome hope of eternity; the Fruit of the Spirit made manifest in my life; and the immeasurable transcendence of God. Fixing my eyes upon such foundational truths will provide me with an eternal perspective that even the most trying circumstances cannot diminish.

Today, put yourself before God's throne and stay there for a while. Ask him to give you eternal eyes and then watch for his revelation. In the midst of your day, look for the deeper meanings, the bigger picture, the hidden truths, and the fingerprints of God. Thank him for such God sightings—those marvelous glimpses of eternity—that stir the soul as we walk by faith. Let us choose to live out Colossians 3:2, which says, "Set your minds on things above, not on earthly things. For you died, and your life is now hidden with Christ in God." We have the mind of Christ, which is to say we have been given the ability, if we stay attuned, to see all of temporal life through the lens of the eternal.

I have you in my heart.

Postscript to ponder: In what areas of your life might God be asking you right now to begin to see through the lens of the eternal; that is, to see your life from God's perspective?

Chapter 6

Dear Lynn:

God did some amazing things in my heart at the retreat. I want to share some of that with you.

God has been teaching me much of his love for me lately. Mostly, that I don't understand it and therefore find it hard to fully accept. God showed me that I have walls around my heart in relationships and, more surprisingly, walls around my heart regarding God.

I was rather convicted and broken! But God did some major excavation on my heart, which is causing me to rest in him. I did not walk away with all the answers to my questions, nor did I figure it out. But, I did surrender and accept my position. That is a very freeing thing.

You can continue to pray for me in this regard. Pray that I would open my heart fully to God and his love for me, that I would accept it and that it would change my view of God and my view of myself.

Love Letter From God

As a bridegroom rejoices over his bride, so will your God rejoice over you.—Isaiah 62:5b

Dear Friends:

What would God say to you if he wrote you a personal love letter? As I thought about this question, I realized that he has written you a love letter called the Word of God. The entire Bible speaks of God's faithful, relentless, lavish love for you. Not long ago, I compiled a group of Bible passages that speak of God's love and gave them to a friend whose heart had been broken. If you find yourself in a place of pain, here is God's love letter to you.

My Beloved Daughter:

I love you with an everlasting love. I want to be your refuge, the person you can run to when you feel lonely, afraid, sad, or rejected. I will hold you in my everlasting arms and comfort you (Deuteronomy 33:27). I know how you are feeling. I am well acquainted with your heart, your thoughts, and your ways, because I created you. You are precious to me beyond description (Psalm 139).

When it is time to give your heart away, do not settle for anything less than my best for you. For I know the plans I have for you and they are good. I desire that you blossom as a beautiful, loved woman and that you experience peace and not misery. I have plans to give you hope and a future if you call upon me and come and talk to me. I will listen to you. You will find me, if you seek me with all your heart (Jeremiah 29:11).

My love is better than the love of any human, because I love you unconditionally, with perfect love. I know you are brokenhearted. I have a special closeness to those who are brokenhearted. I have been brokenhearted myself. I will save those who are crushed in spirit—that is a promise (Psalm 34:18). I am sorry this world is full of so much sorrow and difficulty. It is not what I had intended, but take courage and be of good cheer. I have overcome the world (John 16:33).

I want to be your hiding place. I promise to surround you with deliverance from your fears, loneliness, and feelings of shame. I will teach you the way you should go, who you should spend your time with, and how to live. I will give you counsel and watch over you. My love is unfailing, and my love will surround you if you put your trust in me rather than running into the arms of whatever this world offers—things that will only disappoint you again (Psalm 32:7–8).

I want to give you peace, but my peace is not the world's peace. You are acquainted with a world that strives to find peace through relationships, money, material goods, and physical pleasure, but my peace is not of this world. It is unfailing and eternal; it is available to those who seek it, and it will never fail you. Let me give you my peace (John 14:27).

Where am I, you might ask? Am I far away from you when you are crying in the night? No, I am very near to you, if you would call upon me. I long to fulfill your needs for belonging, acceptance, and love (Psalm 145:18). So come to me, if you are weary and heavy-hearted, and I will give you rest. Do not run to a false lover; run to me. Spend time with me each day and learn about life and love from me, and you will find a sense of well-being for your soul. I will not condemn you. I am gentle and accepting of you just as you are (Matthew 11:28). Rest in me and know I love you and I delight in you. I will quiet you with my love and rejoice over you with singing (Zephaniah 3:17). I want to be your truest friend.

God Almighty, your Heavenly Father

Postscript to ponder: What, if anything, is keeping you from accepting God's love and waiting for his best?

Chapter 7

Dear Lynn:

I know you are wondering ... how are things going in getting over Karl? Well, let me answer that. Great. I haven't heard from him in over a month, so that is always good. His last email was much more formal and distant, which helps my heart but also leaves me filled with sadness at the change in our relationship.

He is still dating Megan, and their relationship is progressing. I predict engagement by the end of the summer. I am learning to live with the loss of our close friendship and, in the process, have learned that I need to guard my heart more when it comes to guy friendships!

Wouldn't you know it, just when I thought my heart was safe and I was doing just fine—single and with no prospects in sight—wham! I start hanging out with a guy and noticing him more and then secretly wishing he would pay me more attention! Argh! Oh, how deceitful is my heart!

I have since withdrawn myself more and have tried my best to put up walls and avoid him, only to protect my own heart and his. This doesn't always work, but it helps. I know it's okay to be attracted to people, which I certainly am with him, but I always end up thinking about a guy all the time, and then I always end up getting hurt. I have started praying for him and then focusing on God alone. I just want to be sure to keep God first. God sure does have a lot of work to do on me.

Guard Your Heart

Above all else, guard your heart, for it is the wellspring of life. Let your eyes look straight ahead, fix your gaze directly before you. Make level paths for your feet and take only ways that are firm.—Proverbs 4:23, 25–26

Dear Friends:

When I was nineteen, I fell hopelessly in love with a redheaded, ruggedly handsome, lacrosse-playing Irish-Italian who lived in my college dorm. I gave him my heart—signed, sealed, and delivered. I handed it over, fragile and full of longing, to one who was not capable of caring for it. Later, when he face-planted me in a messy break-up, my heart was broken into tiny, fractured shards of pain. Any remaining recollections of the Irish-Italian I promptly locked up in my *painful memories* box. I bring up this story not to talk about memory boxes, lacrosse, or Irish-Italians, but because I want to caution you as no one ever cautioned me: guard your heart.

I have found this admonition is of supreme importance for women, whether single or married. Why guard your heart? Guard it from what? And what are the benefits? The heart, the wellspring of life, is the essence of you, the truest you. The heart is more than your emotions and desires. According to Scripture, it is where our deepest thinking takes place; it is where motives and intentions begin; it is where memory is held. The heart is where wisdom is stored, and from the heart, creativity flows.

The Bible has much to say on the state of one's heart. It says the heart can be hardened or softened, pure or perverse, steadfast or faint, sincere or stiff-necked. The heart can be enlarged, deceived, revived, broken, afflicted, made merry, stirred, and humbled. Scripture says the heart searches, ponders, and resolves; it can condemn us, leave us bewildered, and hold secrets. The heart is where grief and laughter reside; it is something we can gain or lose; it is where understanding and wisdom grow. And, if we are in Christ, the Bible tells us the heart can be cleansed, restored, and made new. For the Christian, the heart is where Christ dwells,[1] which makes it central to all of life. In the same way my physical heart dictates how I breathe, my spiritual heart dictates how I live.

While the world says, "Follow your heart," Solomon warns, "Guard your heart," making sure we carefully tend this wellspring of life. This means making sure my affections, thoughts, and intentions push me toward those things that please God. Guarding the heart means to place boundaries on my Self, choosing not to go after everything that entices. There are three areas to consider when guarding your heart.

◆   ◆   ◆

The first is to guard your heart from inappropriate intimacy with men. When I was single, I had an overwhelming desire to bare my soul to the men I dated. This is quite in line with how God created women to be relational and communicative. It is God's design that women want to know and be known, which is why we enjoy conversation and are usually competent communicators. Talking, sharing, and revealing are what women do well. Since there is nothing wrong with this design, the key is appropriateness—sharing my heart with the right person at the right time. When I shared too much too early to the wrong man, it made him responsible for too much information. I put him in an awkward position and usually got hurt, because he was not ready to carry that portion of my heart.

Instead, take the deepest longings of your heart to the living God, who longs to fill you with his presence. Don't guard your heart from God. Pour it out, like King David, in prayers, songs, and poems. Will it feel as satisfying as pouring it out to a man sitting across the table? Perhaps no, perhaps yes, but the result will always bring life.

Another place where it is safe to share your heart is in healthy friendships with women. God gives us friends to share our burdens. Find a safe and trusted friend and divulge your heart to her. Then pray together. Female friendships are a gift from God. When you are married, you will need to share your heart with your husband. At this point, the flipside of the equation is operative: guarding your heart from your husband will only hurt marital intimacy. However, you will need to guard your heart from other men. As a married woman, you may be tempted to flirt with men other than your husband. This may create emotional intimacy; it will grieve God, and hurt you (and your husband). I know this from experience: don't go there!

The second area where I would encourage you to guard your heart is from the enticements of the world. We are surrounded by the world's messages to acquire, amass, update, beautify, manipulate, stray, deceive, improve, covet, and never say no if it feels good. Because God created us with a thirst (see Chapter 9), these imposters of life keep parading themselves before us. Recently, I had the opportunity to visit a friend and stay in her six-million-dollar home. Everything was exquisite and luxuriously appointed. When I returned to my own home, I allowed complaints to consume me. Our home looked worn and shabby in comparison to hers. How grievous those thoughts are to God, who has blessed me immensely with our home.

Finally, guard your heart from the schemes of the devil. The enemy, Satan, is real and seeks to render powerless your service to God through discouragement, depression, and discontentment. These become all-consuming areas of self-focus that cause our paths to grow uneven, our footing unsure. Guard your heart. Don't let Satan get a foothold.[2] When you stray into sin, repent and return to prayer, worship, and Scripture to refocus your gaze on the River of Life.

◆   ◆   ◆

There are at least two benefits to the command to guard your heart. The first will benefit you presently; the second, if you marry.

First, by guarding your heart, you will gain wisdom for today. "Do not forsake wisdom, and she will protect you; love her, and she will watch over you," says the writer of Proverbs 4:6. This Proverb is dedicated to the benefits of wisdom and is where we find the admonition, "Above all else, guard your heart, for it is the wellspring of life." It seems that acquiring wisdom—the skill of living rightly—is connected to what we do with our hearts. If you guard your heart, wisdom will protect you.

Second, by guarding your heart, specifically from inappropriate intimacy with men, you protect your marriage from potential harm. My husband and I know several married people who have given in to affairs, either sexual or emotional. The heart was always the first thing they gave away. Their bodies followed, and their marriages were damaged or destroyed.

Your heart, the wellspring of life, will exude stability, abundance, and beauty if you guard it. This does not mean that you lock it up (like I did) in a carefully built box to protect it from pain—your heart needs to be accessible to the softening touch of God and available to the possibility of marital love—but that you share your heart appropriately with the right persons, using wisdom and discretion. By doing so, God will bless you.

I have you in my heart.

Postscript to ponder: In what areas of your life have you "let down your guard" and need God's help to restore your heart as the wellspring of life?

Chapter 8

Dear Lynn:

I've been noticing that I compare myself to others in a way that doesn't help me embrace my own unique calling and gifts. So the first desire I hope for this year is that Jesus would grow in me new eyes of evaluation, so that I can see myself more clearly, stand more solidly in who God has made me—is making me—and begin living a life faithful to all of that. For sure, it means slowing my pace so there is more margin in my life to set aside for responding to Jesus' promptings.

I feel like I fit in everywhere but don't belong anywhere. This has been a phrase that has come back to haunt me all year, and does describe how I often feel. I want to learn more about allowing myself to be known, even in weakness and failure, and to learn more about developing healthy intimacy with people. I want to develop friendships with single men that remain pure, but are also fun. I want to trust Jesus for his timing on the whole man thing.

Unveiled and Alluring:
Some Thoughts on Biblical, Feminine Beauty

He is taking us somewhere, and along the way he is creating beauty.... God wants to unveil our face, showing the beauty in us to everyone who would see.—Jan Meyers, *The Allure of Hope*

Dear Friends:

We live in a twenty-first-century world that bombards us with its standard of beauty, used to sell everything from cable television to cleansing cream. In our culture, a woman's external beauty is considered her primary means to achieve celebrity, power, and success, but what does the Bible say about beauty? Moreover, what role should beauty play in the life of a woman who seeks to follow God with her whole heart?

Though the world takes credit for creating beauty through avenues of fashion, film, and cosmetics, God is the ultimate author and creator of beauty. This means that God has provided the proper definition and role of beauty through his written word, the Bible. In the book of Genesis, after God created the spectacular universe and called it good, he created man and woman in his own image and called his creation *very good*. The Hebrew text says that God *fashioned* the woman. God was the first fashion designer! You, my friends, have been made particularly beautiful by God's design; you are his fashioned masterpieces.

If men were created to display, among other things, God's attributes of provider and protector, women were indeed created, among other things, to display God's magnificent beauty. When Adam saw the enthralling creature God had given to him, his first response was essentially, "Whoa!"

Not only is God the author of beauty, the Bible is not bashful about noting beautiful women. The Old Testament tells us Sarah was so beautiful Abraham felt he needed to lie that she was his sister.[1] Rebekah's beauty caught Isaac's eye as she approached him across the desert.[2] And Esther's beauty is legendary as a tool God used to save his people from destruction. Yet, as we explore God's heart through Scripture, external beauty is only one facet of God's exquisite design for women.

When God instructed Solomon to build the temple, he gave him detailed specifications to create an immensely beautiful dwelling place to bring glory to God. Solomon used the finest cedar, gold, and gems befitting a king. The New Testament tells us that we, as God's children, are *living* temples. In a similar way, we should take care to prepare our heart, soul, mind, and body as a dwelling place fitting for the King of Kings, with our life's goal to bring glory to God.

I enjoy small rituals to beautify myself on the outside: polish and skin creams, makeup and fragrances, scarves and bright colors. I try for a healthy diet, and plenty of water, rest, and exercise. All that attention to external beauty, however, would be woefully inadequate and sadly misguided if I did not first attend to the inner beauty of my "living temple." The Apostle Peter writes, "Let not your adornment be external only ... but let it be the hidden person of the heart, with the imperishable quality of a gentle and quiet spirit, which is precious in the sight of God."[3]

How does one cultivate inner beauty? Using steps similar to beautifying oneself on the outside, inner beauty consists of cleansing and adornment. Daily cleansing begins with a contrite heart, a choice to come before God to repent of sin and seek forgiveness. "Create in me a clean heart, O God," the psalmist asks. It means to surrender the day to God's agenda. Next comes adornment. Before you put on makeup, jewelry, and clothes, Scripture calls us to *put on a heart of compassion* (Col. 3:12), *put on the full armor of God* (Eph. 6:11), and *put on love* (Col. 3:14). It calls us to *"put on the new self, which in the likeness of God has been created in righteousness and holiness of the truth"* (Eph. 4:24), and *"clothe yourselves with the Lord Jesus Christ"* (Rom. 13:14). If you adorn yourself in this manner, you will exude an aroma called the Fruit of the Spirit, more captivating than any fragrance money can buy, consisting of love, joy, peace, patience, kindness, goodness, faithfulness, gentleness, and self-control.[4]

Finally, don't forget a healthy spiritual diet, which consists of what you choose to feed your mind each day. If you choose to consume the world's music, literature, movies, and magazines, such cultural "junk food" will mar your internal beauty. Alternatively, if you feed upon the things of God (Scripture, as well as music, art, and literature that glorify God) your inner beauty will radiate. Paul writes in Philippians 4:8, "Whatever is true, whatever is noble, whatever is right, whatever is pure, whatever is lovely, whatever is admirable, if anything is excellent or praiseworthy, think about such things."

"True beauty in God's eyes," my friend Lindsay says, "isn't putting me or my body on display, but putting God and his work in me on display. What am I drawing attention to?" It is wonderfully pampering to beautify on the outside; yet more importantly, to beautify within, in order to bring glory to the God who fashioned you. Our beauty as women should always point to the beauty of our Lord.

I have you in my heart.

Postscript to ponder: How are you doing when it comes to cultivating inner beauty? Does your beauty point to the beauty of the Lord?

Chapter 9

Dear Lynn:

As long as I keep looking for my true self in the world of conditional love, I will remain hooked to the world—trying, failing, and trying again. It is a world that fosters addictions because what it offers cannot satisfy the deepest cravings of my heart.

I now know what the deepest craving of my heart is: to not be a part of this world, but walk to the beat of a different drummer and see the world through eyes of compassion and love. No strings attached when it comes to reaching out to others.

Quenching Your Thirst at the River of Life

Our hearts are restless until they find their rest in Thee.
—St. Augustine

The world rings changes; it is never constant but in its disappointments. The world is but a great inn, where we are to stay a night or two, and be gone; what madness is it so to set our heart upon our inn, as to forget our home?—Thomas Watson

Dear Friends:

I never understood the insatiable nature of my thirst until I became a newlywed. During the years I was single, I was acutely aware of my longings, my "deep desires," as musician Chris Rice calls them. It was a thirst not unlike every woman's: to be fully known and loved without conditions; to be understood at the deepest level of my soul; and to be cherished as one who is lovely and valuable. I wanted a champion, someone who would fight for me, and I never wanted to be lonely again. As I said, though, I never understood the nature of this thirst until I got married. As soon as I walked down the aisle and whispered, "I do," I unknowingly transferred this mantel of longings onto my husband's shoulders, fully expecting him to quench my soul-brimming thirst. No one told me this was an untenable expectation; from the start, the man was doomed to disappoint me. And he did.

A few months into our marriage, while he was sleeping next to me in the dark, the familiar emptiness returned that I knew so well as a single woman. I thought the ache would vanish with marriage, yet, like the crashing of a wave, loneliness descended over me with a haunting question: "Is this all there is? I thought it would be better than this." I realized that I was next to the man I loved, yet there was a longing for something more, a thirst at the core of my soul that he could not touch. I now know that thirst is from God, and is *for God*. God created in each of us a holy longing that can only be filled completely by and through the Creator who put it there. We were created with a thirst for beauty, adventure, wholeness, community, and love—each to be satisfied wholly through God alone.

Scripture pulsates with the undercurrents of this thirst. "My soul thirsts for God, for the living God," the psalmist David writes. "Come, all you who are thirsty," the prophet Isaiah beckons. The invitation to "Come!" implies a very important truth. We have a choice to come, or not to come. Not only did God create us with a thirst; he also created us with a choice.

When a Samaritan woman with a dubious past met Jesus while drawing water at a well, Jesus initiated conversation with her, inviting her to ask him for living water. "Everyone who drinks of this (well) water shall thirst again; but whoever drinks of the water that I will give him shall never thirst."[1]

I have a choice. I can drink the all-satisfying living water Jesus offered the woman at the well, which satisfies my thirst; or, *dig my own cisterns* and grab desperate gulps of *worldly water.*

In the Old Testament, a cistern was a place to collect spring water or rain for use as drinking water. These cisterns were usually large pits carved out of a rock or built with bricks, situated in the center of camp. When the families of Israel needed water, they would grab a jug, go to their cistern, and draw water from it. Problem was, the cistern would eventually get cracks in it and no longer hold water. Then the people would leave that cistern and build a new one, depend on it for a while, and move on. These cisterns were valuable assets in the desert, but God portrays them as a picture of self-sufficiency rather than God-dependency.

In the book of Jeremiah, the Lord uses the analogy of the temporary, cracked cistern to describe Israel's wayward rebellion. The Lord said to them:

> My people have exchanged their glorious God for worthless idols! They have forsaken me—the fountain of living water, and they have dug for themselves cracked cisterns that can hold no water at all.[2]

These people were setting aside their relationship with God, the spring of Living Water, for their self-sufficient solutions, their "foreign gods" or idols, that provided temporary gratification until they were discovered to be broken, empty, and worthless. Then, the people moved on to another unstable "cistern" because the grass is always greener, isn't it? I have taken many desperate gulps from empty cisterns during various times in my life, which satisfy only temporarily and then leak out of the gaping God-sized hole in my heart. God provides me refreshing, abundant life, but instead of choosing his life, I grab my canteen and run back and forth to false loves that provide a measure of immediate gratification yet, ultimately, are found to be empty. I am grieved when I take to heart the prophet Jeremiah's exhortation:

> Do not run until your feet are bare and your throat dry. But you said, 'It's no use! I love foreign gods, and I must go after them.'[3]

My helter-skelter running has reaped only bare feet and a dry throat. I avoid the Living Water in order to quench my thirst *my way, in my timing*. These gulps have taken the form of unhealthy relationships, which lead to loneliness; material indulgences that always dissatisfy; addictive behaviors resulting in shame and desperation; and the list goes on. Because I have faced this choice repeatedly, I am learning two life-changing lessons in the process.

First, God in his gracious love for me gave me a thirst *for a purpose*. Soulful thirst has the power to draw me to God in a way that nothing else can. Rather than deny this thirst by ignoring my longings, burying them, or staying too busy to face them, I am learning to embrace the thirst, and even thank God for it. The thirst—that ache or longing I feel in a quiet moment—can point me to the living God every time I honestly acknowledge it in my soul. Does this mean we shouldn't desire marriage or look to a husband to satisfy some of our desires? As the Apostle Paul exclaims, "May it never be!" Marriage is a gift given by God as a picture or foreshadowing of the relationship with the bridegroom, Christ, that we can know in part now and in glorious fullness in eternity. Therefore, desiring marriage is a holy desire, and expecting a level of fulfillment in marriage is a proper expectation. Just don't confuse your earthly groom (with his limited ability to fulfill your longings) with your Heavenly Groom and his infinite, perfect love that will satisfy your desires in full. John Eldredge writes, "Oh, to drink deeply from that fount of which we've had only a sip, to dive into that sea in which we have only waded."[4] This is the Living Water that Jesus makes available to you right now without limit.

Second, when faced with a choice to quench your thirst, don't settle for imposters. Go and drink from the Living Water rather than from the world's faulty cisterns. Let us follow the prophet Micah who writes, "Come, let us go up to the mountain of the Lord."[5] Cultivate a lifestyle of going to the Lord. Stay there, abiding in the presence of Jesus, the River of Life. Don't be deceived. The world's temporary offerings to satisfy your thirst will bring dashed hopes, disappointment, and despair. The Lord's Living Water will bring abundant life, deeply rooted stability, and soulful well-being.

Finally, rest in the ache of your longings, because thirst reminds us to drink deeply from the wellspring of life. "The Spirit and the bride say, 'Come!' And let him who hears say, 'Come!' Whoever is thirsty, let him come; and whoever wishes, let him take the free gift of the water of life."[6] Drink up.

I have you in my heart.

Postscript to ponder: Are you a cistern builder? What is keeping you from drinking living water from the River of Life?

Chapter 10

Dear Lynn:

I had a job interview today. It went great, and I was offered the position. Then my interviewer asked if I thought there would be a problem with the results of the fingerprint test. I found myself wanting to say, "No," but I knew there would be a problem because of my felony.

So I told him all about my criminal background. He still offered me the job, but on the condition that I get this crime closed. In the past, I have tried and the answer always came back No. So, you can imagine the frustration I am feeling right now. The only difference in the past was, I wasn't walking with Christ.

This is a whole new ball game.

The guy who has the potential to be my new boss is a Christian, and he is confident that I would be a positive addition to his staff. The way he didn't judge me about all the stuff in my past was a great blessing, and the fact that he still wants to hire me is an even greater blessing.

God is a God of second chances.

I Will Change Your Name

You will be called by a new name, which the mouth of the Lord will designate. It will no longer be said to you, 'Forsaken,' ... but you will be called, 'My delight is in her.'—Isaiah 62:2b, 4a (NASB)

> I will change your name
> You shall no longer be called
> Wounded, Outcast, Lonely, or Afraid.
> I will change your name,
> Your new name shall be
> Confidence, Joyfulness, Overcoming One,
> Faithfulness, Friend of God, One Who Seeks My Face.
> —D. J. Butler, *I Will Change Your Name*, ©1987 Mercy/Vineyard Publishing (ASCAP).
> Admin. in North America by Music Services o/b/o Vineyard Music USA. All Rights Reserved. Used By Permission.

Dear Friends:

Every Wednesday night my family serves dinner at the Union Gospel Mission, a shelter for homeless men in our city. As the nearly 150 men shuffle through the food line, my job is to serve them dessert. Mostly, I look them in the eye and call them by name. There is Larry, Daniel, Jon, Kendall, Willie, Paul, Tom.... They are patient as I try to remember their names each week.

A name is vitally important: our names represent who we are. In the Old Testament, a name was carefully chosen to identify or reveal a person's character. God has several names in Hebrew, each describing a unique aspect of his nature: Jehovah-Jireh means God Will Provide; El-Shaddai means Almighty; Adonai means Lord; and so on. A name also implies that we belong. Unfortunately, many homeless men feel displaced, without a family or an address, trying to forget a painful past and afraid to glance upon an uncertain future. On the streets, they are shunned by those unwilling to acknowledge their predicament, or the fact that there is a *person* behind the predicament. They struggle with their identity: will they forever be branded "Homeless"?

As a single woman, you may identify with their struggle. Perhaps you are without a community, or dealing with a regrettable past and a murky future. Perhaps you feel defined by the label "Single," shunned by those unsure how to handle your "predicament." Or maybe you've branded yourself with another name.

I have a friend whose name was Angry. That wasn't her real name, of course, but it was her identity. When her father abandoned her at age thirteen to have an affair with her best friend's mother, my friend buried her birth name—a name that means Victory—and became her new name, Angry. When I met her, the Lord had called her to himself as a new follower of Christ, but Angry was the only name she answered to, and every conversation was a reminder of this identity to which she tightly clung. She is learning, however, that the Lord has changed her name. As the Holy Spirit is transforming her into Christlikeness, he is renaming Angry to reflect her new nature: Compassionate, Gentleness, Friend of God.

I have had a name change as well. I am the second of four children, raised in a Christian home. My parents are accomplished, hard-working, and intelligent. When I was a child in their home, they held themselves and their children to high standards. As a result, the message I conjured in my mind (though unintentional by my parents) was that acceptance must be earned through achievement. And so, in high school, I subconsciously named myself Striving. I would strive to maintain good grades, amass friends, load a resume with mountains of activities, and be a good Christian in order to gain acceptance from my family, friends, and church community. I was rewarded for my striving—with honors, popularity, and a crown as Homecoming Queen. This recognition cemented my name, Striving. I continued striving through college and into married life. Then in my early 30s, the Lord began to whisper my new name. I would no longer be called Striving but *Beloved*.

"Cease Striving," he spoke into my heart, "and know that I am God." The Lord used some divinely appointed books to whisper my new name and speak to me of my identity as his Beloved, with a love that is secure, unearned, and unconditional. "I am my beloved's and my beloved is mine," he reminded me in Song of Songs.[1] I am growing into my new name, though, at times, the former name tries to reassert itself with all its wearying expectations.

What names do you call yourself? Wounded, Unstable, Victim, Abandoned, Shunned, Rebellious, Lonely, Afraid, Outcast, Angry, Bitter, Controlling, Ashamed, or Forgotten? If you are God's child, he has already changed your name. He is calling you by a redeemed name, one that he longs for you to take on as your new identity: Beautiful, Chosen, Unafraid, Forgiven, Gracious, Delightful, Blessed, Holy, Blameless, Unashamed, Adopted, and Beloved. These are names promised to you in Scripture.[2] Which of these names is he using right now to beckon you?

Here is more good news. In heaven, our names will change once more. The Lord himself will give each of us another name. It will be a holy, eternal name known in a heavenly language that seals our identity in Christ forever. You can personalize this passage from Isaiah 62:1–4 (NASB):

> For [insert your name] sake I will not keep silent, and for [insert your name] sake I will not keep quiet, until her righteousness goes forth like brightness, and her salvation like a torch that is burning. And the nations will see your righteousness, and all kings your glory; and *you will be called by a new name*, which the mouth of the Lord will designate. You will also be a crown of beauty in the hand of the Lord, and a royal diadem in the hand of your God. It will no longer be said to you, 'Forsaken,' ... but you will be called, 'My delight is in her.'

And Revelation 2:17 (NASB) says,

> To [insert your name] who overcomes, to [insert your name] I will give some of the hidden manna, and I will give [insert your name] a white stone, and a new name written on the stone which no one knows but the one who receives it.

What an incredible promise. Perhaps our heavenly names will reveal some aspect of our eternal nature. Who are you? What is your name? Who is Christ making you to be? Pray for the power to discard your old name and listen as God calls you by your new name. Then, walk in that name, relish its meaning, and embrace its identity.

I have you in my heart.

Postscript to ponder: Is God changing your name? By what new name is he beckoning you?

Chapter 11

Dear Lynn:

I am still grieving the loss of a friendship I thought I had with my former housemate, which I guess never really was at the level I wanted or perceived it to be. There is a line from Rich Mullin's song "Elijah" that seems to sum it up: "There's people been friendly but they'd never be your friends/sometimes this has bent me to the ground."

I have to keep surrendering it. It is getting easier each day. Rich exhorts me, "And if I weep, let me weep as a man who is longing for his home."

God is showing me that these longings to know and be known are misplaced in friends or husbands. Heaven and life everlasting in the garden with my Lord is the only place where this longing can be realized and my heart can truly be satisfied.

And so, I live in the longing and tarry in the tension of Christ's promise fulfilled already, but not yet.

You're Invited

All who are weak
All who are weary
All who are tired
All who are thirsty
All who have failed
All who are broken
Come to the Rock
Come to the Fountain.

—Michael J. Pritzl, *Invitacion Fountain*, ©2000 Mercy/Vineyard Publishing (ASCAP). Admin. in North America by Music Services o/b/o Vineyard Music USA. All Rights Reserved. Used By Permission.

Come to me, all you who are weary and burdened, and I will give you rest. Take my yoke upon you and learn from me, for I am gentle and humble in heart, and you will find rest for your souls.—Matthew 11:28–29

Dear Friends:

An invitation is before you. It is not to a party but to a person. Jesus is inviting you to *come!* It's a simple word packed with unfathomable love and promise. It requires no mustered performance on your part, only a surrendered heart. The invitation is free and longstanding, with no conditions or expiration date.

"Come!" Jesus said. "Come to me, all who are weary and burdened, and I will give you rest." Who could resist such an offer? Yet, I do resist all the time. What keeps me from coming when I am so weary and the invitation is so wondrous? Sometimes my pride whispers, "I'm not desperate enough yet. I'm still quite capable. I will come to him when I have nowhere else to turn." Other times, it is my busyness. "Yes Lord, I want to come! And I will come, but not today. I just can't fit you in." Often, it is the fear of giving up my illusion of control to a mysterious and unpredictable God. "I want to come, Lord, but will it be safe? What will you ask of me? Will it hurt?"

Other issues block my willingness to come. Disobedience. Unconfessed sin. A divided heart that seeks idolatrous affections. Spiritual warfare that attacks me with the accuser's weapons: discouragement, depression, despair, and doubt.

Then there is the enemy's most powerful weapon to keep us from God's presence, one that causes certain paralysis: condemnation. This is the fiery dart that dares to deceive me with the message, "I cannot come because I am shameful. I'm not acceptable to stand before the living God." Don't believe it! Jesus died so you *could* come. He lives that you *would* come. Jesus came for the sinners; he came for the sick. He came for you and me. Jesus is well acquainted with all these roadblocks in my path, yet he still stands patiently at the door of my heart, beckoning, "Come!" I don't have to wait until I'm good enough, pure in thought for an entire day, or faithful enough to please him.

In whatever condition I am in, I can merely call out my pitiful plea, "Jesus, I want to come! Redeem me from the pit! I wish to drink the Water of Life without cost. Lead me to you!" We can utter these words in a prayer, or speak them in our hearts through a song. We can write them in a journal, or in the stanza of a poem. We can cry them out through our tears, or shout them above the roar of the ocean. In whatever way you call out, he will rush to meet you.

"I waited patiently for the Lord; he turned to me and heard my cry," writes King David. "He lifted me out of the slimy pit, out of the mud and mire; he set my feet on a rock and gave me a firm place to stand. He put a new song in my mouth, a hymn of praise to our God."[1] Jesus calls himself the Fountain, the River of Life, and the Living Water. Thirsty hearts will thirst no more if they come to him.

"Behold," Jesus says, "I stand at the door and knock; if anyone hears my voice and opens the door, I will come in to him, and will dine with him, and he with me."[2] Come as you are.

I have you in my heart.

Postscript to ponder: What is keeping you from responding to Christ's invitation to come and enjoy intimate friendship with him?

Chapter 12

Dear Lynn:

You know I've been struggling for a long time with my sexuality, and it has just gotten worse. I met an incredible person recently, and it is not a *he*.

I am in love. She is an incredible woman and my head is spinning. Why can't I love women *and* love God?

Sexual Temptation and the Question of Same-sex Love

There is a sense in which sexual sins are different from all others. In sexual sin we violate the sacredness of our own bodies, these bodies that were made for God-given and God-modeled love, for "becoming one" with another.—1 Corinthians 6:18 (MSG)

The Fall has fallen on us and we are fallen.—Andrée Seu

Dear Friends:

In response to the question on the previous page—whether my friend can love God *and* love women sexually—it is important to discover what God says about homosexual love. May these words of truth and love offer guidance to those struggling with lesbian attractions, or to anyone trapped in an inappropriate sexual relationship, or tempted by sexual sin.

> My Dear Friend,
> You shared with me that you recently slept with a married woman, and you wanted to know what I thought about that. What I think is much less important than what God thinks about your choices, because he loves you so greatly.
> In the Old Testament, a woman who slept with a married woman would be guilty of a trio of sins: fornication, adultery, and homosexuality. According to Hebrew law, you would be stoned to death.
> Jesus met a woman in a similar situation in the New Testament,[1] but the outcome was quite different. As the woman stood in the center of the crowd with the religious leaders jeering at her, Jesus said, "All right, stone her. But let those who have never sinned throw the first stone."

When the accusers heard this, they slipped away one by one, until only Jesus and the woman remained.

"Where are your accusers?" Jesus asked. "Didn't even one of them condemn you?"

"No," she answered.

"Neither do I," Jesus replied. "Go and sin no more."

I will not be throwing any stones at you in this letter, but I will implore you to consider Jesus' words, *"Go, and sin no more."* You said you didn't want me to back you into a corner. Actually, you have backed yourself into a corner. My intention is to show you the way of escape from a path you are on that only leads to destruction. Not yet, perhaps—it is still deliciously new—but eventually.

You know this path already. As a former lesbian, you walked this path for many years until the Lord plucked you from a destructive lifestyle of homosexuality and set you free into his life of salvation. You tasted the sweetness of peace, freedom, and pure love for the first time in your life. Now, the enticing temptation for a woman has led you back down the old path. You say your head is spinning. You are deliriously infatuated. You've asked, *Why can't I love women sexually and love God?* You cannot: these two loves are mutually exclusive. One cannot exist if the other exists.

The Lord said, "If you love me, obey my commandments."[2] It is a clear statement, but he restates it later for emphasis: "When you obey me, you remain in my love." Our love for God is proved in our obedience toward him. We show our love for God by keeping his commandments—every one of them, not just the ones that are convenient or easy. It says in the book of First John, "If someone says, 'I belong to God,' but doesn't obey God's commandments, that person is a liar and does not live in the truth."[3] These words are difficult to hear, but God wrote them for our good.

So what does God say about same-sex love? Self-proclaimed followers of Jesus who are choosing homosexuality have rationalized the Bible's commands on this subject to support their lifestyle choice. Yet it is hard to dispute Romans 1, where God refers to same-sex love with words such as "impurity," "dishonoring," "degrading passions," "women exchanged the natural function for that which is unnatural," "men with men committing indecent acts," "depraved," and worthy of "due penalty for their error."[4]

Scripture is also quite black and white in I Corinthians 6:9: "Do you not know that the unrighteous shall not inherit the kingdom of God? Do not be deceived; neither fornicators, nor idolaters, nor adulterers, nor effeminate, nor homosexuals …" The Bible makes it clear that you cannot love women sexually and love God at the same time. To love women sexually is in direct disobedience to God's will. You have to make a choice. You must serve one master or the other. You can choose to serve yourself and try to satisfy your cravings in your own way, or you can choose to serve God and surrender your longings to his way. One path brings emotional and spiritual death; the other, emotional and spiritual life.

If the right path seems clear from Scripture, why does sexual sin look so attractive? God designed sexual love to touch us at the core of our body, soul, and spirit. He created sexual pleasure to be compelling because it is a *symbol of the perfect union* we can experience with Christ in part today, and fully in eternity. Sex within a monogamous marriage is a picture of oneness between the bride of Christ (us, as part of the church) and the Bridegroom (Christ). Of course sexual intimacy is attractive; God wouldn't have designed it any other way. Then sin entered the picture and deceived us, distorting God's beautiful plan of married sexual love. We are now deluded into thinking we must grab sexual pleasure, intimacy, and fulfillment for ourselves any way we can get it. We are marring his symbol of spiritual intimacy with cheap imitations: pornography, affairs, same-sex relationships, premarital sex, and well-developed fantasy lives. Is God grieved? We cannot begin to conceive the depth of his grief.

Throughout our lives, we are all tempted to sin in many areas, including sexual temptation. You might be attracted to women for the rest of your life, and this will be the primary battle you will continue to fight as a follower of Christ. *Battling temptation is not sin*; choosing to act upon, indulge in, or carry out the temptation is the point when it becomes sin. The Bible tells us we will all be tempted; even sinless Jesus was tempted. Scripture instructs us to fight most temptation with the Sword of the Spirit, which is the Word of God.[5] However, regarding *sexual temptation*, the Bible instructs us to use a different tactic: Flee. If you run from sexual temptation, you will be spared the pain and destruction that is always the result of breaking one of God's commandments and stepping outside of his will.

> Run away from sexual sin! No other sin so clearly affects the body as this one does. For sexual immorality is a sin against your own body. Or don't you know that your body is a temple of the Holy Spirit, who lives in you and was given to you by God? You do not belong to yourself, for God bought you with a high price. So you must honor God with your body.[6]

My friend, you have opened the door of temptation to sexual sin, and you want to linger there. You have walked down a path that leads away from God. For now, you are not sure you want to turn around. For now, you love the way this relationship makes you feel. I understand how fiercely our feelings want to drive our behaviors, but there is one problem. When you gave your life to God through Christ, you gave up your right to call the shots. Your body is no longer your own; you were bought with a price. Jesus paid a steep price with his own blood so you could have a relationship with God, the Father. So now, you are to honor God with your body. That means he calls the shots, and you must bring under his control every craving and desire you have. This is not an easy endeavor. Being a disciple of Jesus is often difficult. It means I cannot satisfy every craving; I cannot follow every whim that looks attractive or pleasurable. I have to use discipline and self-control—not popular concepts in today's culture. I follow the Master because I believe that when he directs my life, it is always for my own good, and the results are life producing.

You have a choice to make. You cannot pass off this choice and blame your parents, past abusers, or the church for falling short. The choice is this: you can either continue calling the shots on the path you are on, or you can confess your misstep, turn around, flee sexual temptation, and run into the arms of the living God who longs to take you back. By staying on the path you're on and continuing a lifestyle of known sin, you have made your choice. I cannot condone your lifestyle choice to succumb to the temptation of a same-sex relationship because I know it will hurt you. As the Lord's servant, I can only speak the truth in love. I am learning to hate sin in my life, not only because God hates sin, but also because I have experienced the painful consequences of choosing my own way. I want so much for you to hate sin in your life as well. Sin separates me from God, but when I confess my sin and repent—turn around—from it, I am restored into God's presence. No sin is beyond God's forgiveness. If so, the cross would not have been enough.

You say you feel agitated over what to do with this relationship. You cannot sleep, nor can you eat. I don't doubt it. You will never find peace in places of deception. The payment for sin is always death.[7] No, you won't be struck by a lightning bolt. Choosing to remain in disobedience to God brings a slower, insidious death. It starts with restlessness, frustration, and loneliness. It eventually evolves into anger, blaming-shifting, cynicism, and bitterness. The result is a hardened heart, which takes the appearance of a hard-edged personality masking despair below the surface. I have never met a person living in sin who consistently displays the Fruit of the Spirit: love, joy, peace, patience, kindness, goodness, faithfulness, gentleness, and self-control.

You say that God has been silent in your life. May I suggest that perhaps by your choices you have silenced him? Consider the last time you opened his Word and said (as Samuel did), "Speak, Lord, for your servant is listening." He will silently wait for you to invite him to speak. He awaits your choice. He lavishly loves you and hopes you will make the right one. I hope that as well. I want you to experience peace, stability, and life. Those things are found on one path alone.

I have you in my heart.

Postscript to ponder: Is there any door to sexual sin you have opened or are considering opening? What is God saying to you right now regarding that choice?

Chapter 13

Dear Lynn:

Since I have been a Christian, I have always wanted to serve in some type of missions work. When I first started my faith journey, I knew I wanted to be a staff member with a college campus ministry. I prevented myself from pursuing this due to a lack of faith in being able to raise support. Not having a Christian family or any adults close to me when I was younger made me decide that God was not big enough to provide for me. I now know that to be a false statement.

So, since my faith is stronger, I have decided to pray about being a missionary. I am in the first stages of this pursuit, seeing if this is what God has been telling me for the past fifteen years. I have been doing a Bible study, and everything I am hearing points to missions.

Eight Words to Change Your Life

I am determined to be absolutely and entirely for Him and for Him alone.—Oswald Chambers

Dear Friends:

In the last few years, eight simple words have changed the focus and tenor of my spiritual journey. I first whispered these words to God six years ago on an airplane. I was wedged between two executives on a packed flight from San Jose to Portland. I had just spent the weekend with a group of single women at an oceanside retreat. The Lord arranged it so that I could teach from the Bible and share my life with these women. Throughout the weekend, he gave me encouraging words to speak to many teachable hearts. For perhaps the first time in my life, I felt like a vessel expressly used by God for his purposes and keenly aware of his presence. It was a sweet experience, and I wanted more of it.

And so, as I sat buckled between two oblivious passengers on that short flight homeward, my heart ached from having to say goodbye to these women. Yet, at the same time, my heart soared in knowing God had clarified my calling. As I reflected on the life I was returning to in Spokane, I longed for the Lord to use me in my own community. I decided at that moment that I would do anything God called me to do, go anywhere, and say anything, if I could again experience his presence in such a palpable way as I had that past weekend. In the squished solitude of the airplane seat, a prayer welled up in me, formed by the Spirit, which burst upon my conscience. It has become my life prayer: "Teach me! Fill me! Send me! Use me!"

In the Bible, young Samuel uttered a similar prayer. Upon his birth, his mother, Hannah, dedicated Samuel to God's service. As a young boy, Samuel lived in the temple as an assistant to Eli the priest. Of his early years, the Bible says, "Samuel grew up in the presence of the Lord." His first encounter with God came some years later, "as Samuel grew taller and gained favor with the Lord." He was sleeping in the tabernacle when he heard someone calling his name: "Samuel, Samuel." Thinking Eli had called him, he ran to Eli and said, "Here I am." But Eli had not called, and Samuel went back to bed. The Lord called Samuel a second and third time before Samuel realized who was speaking. When the Lord again called, "Samuel, Samuel," the boy replied, "Here I am, speak Lord, for your servant is listening." From that moment on, the Lord spoke frequently to Samuel and used him mightily to do his work. Samuel became one of Israel's greatest prophets and was privileged to anoint Israel's first king.

Samuel waited on the Lord. When the Lord called, Samuel answered, listened, and was available for the Lord's directive. He asked the Lord to speak and then obeyed his voice. The result, the Bible says, is that "the Lord was with Samuel as he grew up, and he let none of his words fall to the ground."[1]

If you are ready for a life of spiritual adventure and intimacy with God, consider praying a prayer similar to Samuel's: Here I am, speak Lord. Your servant is listening. Teach me. Fill me. Send me. Use me. These eight words are rich with implications.

Teach me! One of the jobs of the Holy Spirit is to expound the teachings of Jesus in our hearts; as Psalm 16:11 says, "to make known the path of life." God wants you to know him through his Word. If the cry of your heart is *Teach me,* God will answer that prayer abundantly and with certitude. You can make the Psalmist's prayer your own: "Teach me your way, O Lord, and I will walk in your truth; give me an undivided heart, that I may fear your name."[2] But we don't learn God's Word through osmosis. It is a process of study and discipline. A student needs a teacher: if we become students of the Word, we will learn from the Master.

Fill me! This prayer was familiar to the Apostle Paul who, throughout the Epistles, fervently prayed that the saints be "filled with joy," "filled with the knowledge of his will," "filled with comfort," "filled with the fullness of God," and "filled with the Spirit." The Holy Spirit is given to followers of Christ for several purposes. The Spirit gives us comfort, guidance, and counsel; he reveals truth and prays on our behalf prayers we cannot utter. The Holy Spirit interprets the life and nature of Christ. He imparts to us what Oswald Chambers calls "the quickening life of Jesus." If you want Jesus' nature to be worked into your being, ask God to fill you with a fresh imparting of Jesus through the Spirit. Then yield to the Spirit's work in your life.

Send me! Uttering these words won't necessarily find you on a one-way trip to the mission field, but they might. These words should not be confined to the call of missionaries, but to all saints who wish to be sent to do God's work. Usually, I am busy telling God where I would like to go, but when I pray the words, "Send me!" and then watch how my day unfolds, I discover that God's agenda is very different from mine and always life enhancing. God may send me to talk to a discouraged friend, or send me to my knees to pray. He may send me to a party to be a light among lonely people, or to bed to replenish my body with much-needed sleep. Occasionally, God's agenda for me involves some kind of sensational, limelight opportunity. Mostly, though, because God loves *people*, his agenda seems to involve some menial task or obscure duty—like drying dishes or folding bulletins—where I have the chance to care for someone in the process. It makes no difference whether God sends us to do the tiniest thing or the grandest thing. Whatever God's program, may we be ready for his send-off.

Use me! Christians are vessels containing the life of Christ, to be poured out to a broken and hurting world. How sad when I am an *unused* vessel, a ceramic pot that sits on the upper shelf, *looking* useful but actually gathering dust. When you give God permission to use you—what the Bible calls sanctification—the results are wondrous and memorable.

God desires that you partner with him in ministering to a darkened generation.[3] He does not *need you* in order to advance his kingdom, but desires that you choose to be a part of his bigger story in order that you may know him and experience him as he accomplishes his work through you. As you begin to taste the experience of the Lord using you, flaws and all, you will say "yes" more willingly with each new day.

Are you ready for adventure as a servant of Jesus Christ? Pray these eight words earnestly, and then watch what happens next. You don't have to be old enough, or wise enough, or married to utter these eight words. You don't have to have your educational goals figured out, be settled in a home, financially secure, astutely prepared for your next career move, or spiritually super-sized. You need only to surrender your will—"an absolute and irrevocable surrender of will," writes Oswald Chambers—and cry out to God the prayer of your heart, "Have your way with me."

I have you in my heart.

Postscript to ponder: Is anything preventing you from crying out to God, "Have your way with me"?

Chapter 14

Dear Lynn:

I am in a state of spiritual sluggishness, weariness, and apathy. I feel partially asleep. I have neither passion for God nor compassion for people.

The Lord seems to be gently probing at some of my "internal disabilities," whispering my need to cultivate gentleness and humility; to bear all things and forgive others; to be moderate, charitable, and gracious. I don't like seeing my shortcomings. It makes me like myself less, on both the outside and the inside. Because I do not like myself, I'm not doing a very good job of loving others. Instead, I turn to what pleases me and brings me quick comfort: spending money, controlling others, eating and drinking too much, disappearing into solitude, entertaining fantasies. In this struggle against myself, I have lashed out in anger toward others, enjoying the fleeting feeling of being in control, though I am very out of control and feel ashamed.

Does the Lord really promise that he is renewing my inner self? Can I really not lose heart? He has asked that I make my requests known to him, so here they are: I want to be gentle and humble. I want the power, in Jesus' name, to rejoice—to celebrate him—even when my "self" doesn't feel like it. I want to dismiss my feelings and walk by faith. I want him to lead me from this place of spiritual sluggishness to a place of spiritual restoration.

Spiritual Slump

You are my lamp, O Lord; the Lord turns my darkness into light. With my God I can scale a wall.—2 Samuel 22:29, 30b

There is something strangely wakeful about desperation.—Randy Stonehill

Dear Friends:

"In the midst of the murkiness, let me find you." That has been my prayer these past few months as I have found myself, like my friend in the accompanying letter, paralyzed by a spiritual slump. I have been dealing with chronic back pain, closing myself off to all but pain management. The Lord has been there, waiting silently, but I have been unwilling to go to him. He has always been there, close enough to "feel my breath," as my favorite musician, Chris Rice, sings, but I have moved away from God. Worship music brought me back. Songs of truth, sung in quiet contemplation, cut through the fog and made straight a pathway to the heavenlies. I am grateful, since my past seasons of spiritual "slumpiness" have lasted much longer.

Inasmuch as the disciple of Jesus encounters soaring moments of spiritual ecstasy, mountaintop experiences, and spiritual "highs," the reality is that she will experience the darker valleys, the deserts of dryness, and the spiritual slumps. If you are encountering such a season, there is no magic wand to wave or potent pill to swallow to draw you back into spiritual fervor, yet God says, "I will never leave you nor forsake you,"[1] so even in your slump, he is there.

Time spent alone in solitude or a change of circumstances often leads me back into an awareness of God's presence. Other times, I must make a conscious choice to draw near to God, whether the inspiration is there or not. For me, that "drawing near" is the choice to *worship*.

Consider a palace, where God is in the throne room. Outside the throne room are the king's courts. Surrounding his courts are the gates to the Celestial City. The Bible uses such metaphors in Psalm 100 to describe our journey into the presence of the King of Kings. The best way out of a spiritual slump is to have an encounter with this king.

Psalm 100:4 says, "Enter his gates with thanksgiving...." The first step through the divine gates into the presence of God is by the deliberate choice to give thanks. Why? Because the declaration of thanks to God is counter to our natural inclination. Giving thanks requires a deliberate denial of Self and a humility before God to utter words of appreciation. Thanksgiving reminds me that there is a God, and I am not he.

If pride and selfishness are our natural tendencies in the flesh, then humility and thanksgiving to God are *supernatural* in the Spirit. "May the words of my mouth and the meditation of my heart be pleasing in your sight, O Lord," says Psalm 19:14. We need to give thanks regardless of whether or not we feel thankful.

Feelings are often our least trustworthy advisors. Our *will* to be thankful can act separately from our *feelings* of thankfulness. I use a journal to give thanks, writing down the gifts God has given me for which I am grateful: Jesus, salvation, eternal life, hope, friendships, and circumstances—good and bad, which he is free to alter at any time. The moment we give thanks, a supernatural process begins. We enter his gates and begin to glimpse the previously murky divine kingdom before us where the king dwells in his holy courts.

"Enter his courts with praise." After we have given thanks, Psalm 100 tells us we can go further into God's presence, past the gates, and into the King's courts through the vehicle of praise. Praise is different from thanksgiving. Praise is the choice to enumerate—or list—the attributes of God. If I praise you, I will say to another: "She is friendly, kind, and funny. She is a great listener. She has wisdom and insight." When we offer praise to God, we consciously remind ourselves of God's attributes. He is majestic and sovereign, full of grace and mercy; he is faithful and unchanging. He is just, good, and full of beauty. His love endures forever. Such expressions of praise ready my heart to be in his presence; they humble me and put Self in its proper place. Praise realigns my gaze "not on what is seen, but on what is unseen."[2]

After offering thanksgiving and praise, we find ourselves in the King's throne room, ever closer to God's presence. Does he hide behind the veil in the throne room like the Wizard of Oz, with bluster and bombastic consternation? Not at all. In fact, at the moment of Jesus' death on the cross, the temple veil tore in two, a profound symbol of the believer's newly gained access to God because of the love of Jesus, the High Priest, and his ultimate sacrifice as the Lamb of God. You and I have direct access to the King straight into his throne room. Let these words comfort you:

> This High Priest of ours understands our weaknesses, for he faced all of the same temptations we do, yet he did not sin. So let us come boldly to the throne of our gracious God. There we will receive his mercy, and we will find grace to help us when we need it.[3]

We need grace to help us more than ever when we are in a spiritual slump, because we have an enemy that will do everything in his power to keep us away from God. One of Satan's tactics is *shame*, the voice inside you that says, "You're pathetic. You've fallen too far away this time. He will never take you back." Romans 8:1, however, clearly states the truth: If you are a Christian, you are not condemned; the cross has forever washed away your shame. You are a daughter of the King, and God is your "Abba," a term of endearment, which essentially means "daddy." You can approach Abba with confidence and experience his love when you first choose to "enter his gates" and "enter his courts" through the vehicles of thanksgiving and praise. By doing so, you will find that you have moved past spiritual slumpiness into the presence of a tender God.

I have you in my heart.

Postscript to ponder: Are you condemning yourself for being in a spiritual slump? Choose instead to offer thanksgiving and praise as you wait for God to lead you through the murkiness of your circumstances into his throne room.

Chapter 15

Dear Lynn:

I am alarmed: my mother is going to be sixty next year—a widow with a very limited social network, and children who barely speak to her. I am her family, and yet we don't function as a family. Her life is going to work, coming home, and trying to maintain a house by herself, scraping for a sense of meaning, or mattering to someone.

My grandmother, who lived with us when I was growing up, was widowed. Under our roof, she faded for lack of affection and respect, lack of honor. She was lonely, with few friends, wounded often by our insensitivity or belligerence, and not very known or able to give her heart away. These are the women I am terrified of becoming.

I am not afraid of remaining single. I am afraid of increasingly not knowing how to function with anyone as family, of growing increasingly reticent toward letting my heart take the risk of loving other people and of letting myself be known.

Longing for Intimacy

> I want to know you, I want to be where you are. I want to touch you, I want to have your heart.—Jamie Archer, *I Want to Know You*, ©2003, Spokane, WA. All Rights Reserved. Used By Permission.

> God is so vastly wonderful, so utterly and completely delightful that He can, without anything other than Himself, meet and overflow the deepest demands of our total nature.—A. W. Tozer, *The Pursuit of God*

Dear Friends:

I am no music historian, but I have noticed a groundswell of longing expressed in the lyrics of today's Christian songwriters. I am not diminishing the grand and glorious hymns of old, but I also enjoy contemporary music because it pulsates with an honest cry for intimacy with the living God that ascends straight to his heavenly throne. I am stirred by these songwriters' passion for God.

Men and women have always had a longing for intimacy. Look at an excerpt from Thomas à Kempis' *The Imitation of Christ*, completed in 1441. He writes, "O God, living Truth, unite me to Yourself in everlasting love! Often I am wearied by all I read and hear. In You alone is all that I desire and long for." God created us with such longings. I am encouraged that so many of today's followers of Jesus are eager, above all else, to express their spiritual longings through music, poetry, and art in a way that is nakedly vulnerable to God. Such longing for intimacy is a universal need, a need at the core of our nature for a relationship that provides the reality of knowing and being known. The whole purpose of the disciple's life is to enter into this type of relationship with God, the Father, through Jesus Christ, to search for him and discover that he offers the closest and dearest association we can know.

Because God knows we need earthly examples of spiritual realities, God designed love between a husband and wife—expressed physically in the sexual relationship—to be a picture of the spiritual intimacy God desires with each of us, whether married or single. This is a perfectly vulnerable, wholly trustworthy, and naked-but-not-ashamed intimacy before him and with him.

God also paints a picture of intimacy with himself using the gift of human friendships, which allow us to experience tender affection between each other called *phileo* love. He gives us deep friendships on earth as a picture of the friendship he longs to have with us. "I have called you friends," Jesus told his disciples. You probably enjoy a certain level of intimacy with someone you consider your best friend. You know her because you know what makes her tick. You know her passions and her longings. You know what saddens her and what brings her exceeding joy. You know those moments when she has ached and cried. You know the times she has loved greatly, whether or not it has been returned. You know what makes her smile and laugh aloud. You know her thoughts before she expresses them. You know her heart. This is intimacy, the depth of relationship God longs to have with you.

As a side note, there can also be unhealthy intimacy between women. Sadly, a reality I see today is for a woman to look to another woman for fulfillment of her longings in an inappropriate way. I have observed what begins as a healthy, God-given friendship between two women stray beyond the borders of godly friendship into inappropriate intimacy and sexual behavior. Such responses are fueled by a keen awareness of a longing inside, but an unwillingness to be obedient to God's provision of himself to satisfy that longing. These women are short-circuiting God's plan of providing them with his agape intimacy and, instead, are grabbing for a cheap imitation. Remember those empty cisterns? Don't mistake the longing for intimacy, *which only God can satisfy,* with inappropriate intimacy with a woman. This sin grieves God and results in pain and emptiness.

The Lord longs to fulfill your needs for intimacy with himself. Proverbs 3:32 (NASB) states, "[The Lord] is intimate with the upright." Delve deeper into the Hebrew root of the word for *intimate* and you will find that it involves the *bestowing of God's secret counsel* and *confidentiality.* The upright woman who walks in the fear of the Lord will have God's secret counsel. She will enjoy his companionship in a confidential and deeply satisfying relationship. Jesus longed for intimacy with the children of Israel, who symbolically represent us—the church, God's family. He expressed this desire in a heartfelt cry as he sat above the city of Jerusalem and lamented their rebellion: "O Jerusalem, Jerusalem … how often I have longed to gather your children together, as a hen gathers her chicks under her wings, but you were not willing."[1]

Are you willing to let Jesus gather you under his wings? Are you willing to develop intimacy with God? It fills the Lord's heart with joy whenever a disciple desires to grow in intimacy with him, to search him and by listening to him, come to know him; to talk and walk with him, and take notice of his smile. To know what grieves him and what delights him. To enjoy him forever. Once we experience such intimacy with God through Christ, we notice we can be alone and not be lonely; we don't need sympathy or constant affirmation; and we can "run and not grow weary" when it comes to serving and pouring ourselves into the lives of others. As we grow in intimacy with God through Christ, we leave behind an unmistakable fragrance, what the Bible calls a "life-giving perfume."[2]

Oswald Chambers states it well: "The saint who is intimate with Jesus will never leave the impression of himself, but only the impression that Jesus is having unhindered way, because the last abyss of his nature has been satisfied by Jesus. The only impression left by such a life is that of the strong calm sanity that Our Lord gives to those who are intimate with Him."[3] I want that strong calm sanity in my life. Jesus, have your unhindered way with me.

I have you in my heart.

Postscript to ponder: Does God know all your longings and places of thirst? Pour out your heart to him, and then listen for his secret counsel.

Chapter 16

Dear Lynn:

I have a boyfriend! Although this isn't common knowledge, I appreciate your ability not to spread rumors, and thus I tell you the great news. Our first "official date" will be this Friday, marking four weeks of us knowing each other. We are both still awestruck at how similar our personalities are, how well we communicate, how well we laugh together, and how many eccentricities we share.

Although we are still getting to know each other, I cannot deny God's sovereignty in this matter.

Ten Questions Before Saying "I Do"

> If any of you lacks wisdom, he should ask God, who gives generously to all without finding fault, and it will be given to him.—James 1:5

Dear Friends:

I broke off a seven-year relationship because of ten questions. I did not set out to write these questions, nor did I expect to use them to walk away from someone I believed was the love of my life. I did, however, ask God for wisdom as I contemplated the future of our relationship. Rather quickly, God began to compose this list of ten questions in my mind. Some of the questions came to me by way of close friends; others during quiet times of reflection. As each question was articulated, I wrote it down until it seemed the list was complete. When I finally sat down to evaluate my serious relationship and whether to say, "I do," these questions brought to light some glaring red flags. I still cared for this man, but I broke it off. It was extremely painful, but he wasn't the one I was to marry.

If you hope to marry, or are in a serious relationship where you are discussing marriage, it is important to come up with some objective guidelines, a mental profile, of the type of man you will choose. Suppose you believe this person could be "the one" with whom you want to share your life. How will you know? What are you looking for?

These guidelines are not about height, weight, or hair color, but rather the character qualities necessary to form a solid, enduring marriage. Now is the time to decide the standards God wants you *to be* and *to marry*, before you stand at the altar. Here are the questions God had me compile in deciding upon my future husband. Perhaps they will help you form your own marriage guidelines and lead you to certainty in making one of the most important decisions of your life.

1. *Is this person as spiritually committed as I am?* The guy I came close to marrying went to church, but placed a low priority on his daily relationship with Christ. The components of faith—prayer, Bible study, and Christian community—seemed to be more important to me than to him. We would have faced many struggles in our marriage because of these differences in our faith values. The most important aspect of a Christian marriage is that both partners hold Jesus Christ as their highest priority. Like a triangle, with a man and woman at the bottom corners and Christ at the apex, the closer the two move toward Christ, the closer they move toward each other. The Bible advises, "Do not be yoked together (don't team up) with unbelievers."[1] This verse uses the analogy of trying to plow a field with an unequal pairing, such as an ox and donkey, yoked together. The plowing will not go smoothly; their size, strength, and dispositions are unsuitable. This command tells us not to be bound in marriage to unbelievers, but two Christians can also be unequally yoked if they do not share the same spiritual priorities, if they are not able to "spur one another on toward love and good deeds."[2]

2. *Does this person challenge me spiritually?* When I dated my husband, I found a noticeable difference from previous men I had dated because Jeff challenged me to wholeheartedly pursue God. We memorized Scripture together, attended church as a couple, and encouraged each other in personal Bible study. As I grew in my love for this man, I grew in my love for God. This is how God intends marriage to be: a picture of Christ's love for the church. There is something very inspiring in a marriage when two people encourage each other toward spiritual maturity. If you are striving to challenge your partner spiritually, ask yourself if he is doing the same for you. Does he encourage you to daily spend time with God, read the Bible, and pray? Do you inspire each other toward godliness?

3. *Does this person take responsibility for controlling our physical relationship and respecting my sexual boundaries?* I once

knew a beautiful single woman who rarely spent a Saturday night alone. However, the men she dated were mainly interested in seeing how far they could go with her physically. She got tired of playing referee, blowing the proverbial "whistle" when things got heated. As a result, she developed low self-esteem and an unhealthy perspective of God's purposes in sexuality. This counsel is as sound as the day it was written: "It is God's will that you should be sanctified: that you should avoid sexual immorality; that each of you should learn to control his own body in a way that is holy and honorable."[3] In measuring a man for marriage, ask yourself: Does he respect the limits I have set physically? Does he honor me by honoring my body?

4. *Does this person respect me in other areas as well?* Before marrying, I observed lots of couples and how they treated each other in public. It made me cringe when I saw one spouse criticize the other, usually through sarcasm. The person you marry needs to respect you in all areas—your thoughts, feelings, background, family, goals, priorities—and show that respect to you publicly. He should treat you with honor in front of others. Healthy marriages consist of partners who mutually respect each other and communicate that respect both verbally and nonverbally.

5. *Do I respect this person?* Respect for your husband does not magically appear once you say your wedding vows. It must become self-evident in dating. My friend Lisa found several areas in her fiancé's life that troubled her, but she believed that once they were married, the respect would follow. Now, several years later, respect for her husband is still elusive. Because she struggles to respect him, it affects their intimacy, communication, and trust.

6. *Am I compatible with this person?* This is not a question of sexual compatibility. There is no need to try out sexual compatibility with your partner before marriage. God made men and women remarkably compatible. Rather, how well-matched are

your goals for faith, careers, lifestyle, hobbies, children, ministry, and finances? When I was single, my picture of marriage was a house in suburbia, a hot shower in the morning, and clean feet before bed. I once dated a person who planned to be a Peace Corps volunteer. His goal was to live among the Guatemalan people in clay huts. I did not share his vision and decided to let him find a woman who did (and he found her). While it is true that no two people are perfectly compatible—solid marriages are based on commitment—your marriage is enhanced if you share goals and values that are similar and are willing to support each other toward reaching them.

7. *Do my friends and family affirm our relationship?* My parents were uneasy about a couple of the people I dated. I am so glad I took into account their concerns. Opinions matter from the important people in your life—parents, a trusted friend, a pastor—regarding the man you will marry. In determining God's will for your future as a couple, it is helpful to hear how others view your relationship. Do they enjoy being with you together? Do they believe you bring out the best in each other? Do they see you being yourself with this man? Your parents and close friends know you and see aspects of your relationship you may not see. Listen to them.

8. *Does this person make important decisions based on prayer?* My parents have been married fifty years. I asked them what single factor has kept their marriage strong and they answered unequivocally: prayer. Fifteen years into their marriage (coincidentally at the same time I entered adolescence), they started praying together every morning. They brought to God their struggles, fears, and concerns. This daily routine has sustained them for decades. Prayer is a stabilizing force in a Christian's life: a marriage without prayer is shaky. Carefully observe whether your partner makes prayer a priority in his daily life. As a side note, take care to avoid lengthy prayer times together during the early stages of a dating relationship. Why? Prayer is an intimate activity and can create emotional attachments too

quickly, or create a premature sense of closeness before a solid foundation has been established.

9. *Is this person teachable?* My friend Audrey winced from across the table as she witnessed her boyfriend's messy table manners. She made a note of this on her mental checklist. Mitch had one overriding quality, however, that caused Audrey to marry him despite his less-than-desirable eating habits: Mitch was teachable. He earnestly wanted to be God's man, learn the skills of gracious living, and gain wisdom. If you are considering marrying someone, you should be willing to live with him *as is*, with no checklist for changes once you are married. After the honeymoon, only God can change your mate. Yet *being teachable;* that is, being willing to work on changing undesirable habits, is an important characteristic to look for in a partner. You may not be able to change the minor indiscretions of your spouse, but if he has a teachable heart, they are easier to accept and overlook.

10. *Do I feel peace that this is God's man for me?* Throughout my dating adventures, I prayed for wisdom that my choice for a husband would be pleasing to God. When I met Jeff, I asked God to give me peace regarding our future. The peace God gave me filled my heart, and we confidently began planning our wedding. It says in Philippians 4:6,

> Do not be anxious about anything, but in everything, by prayer and petition, with thanksgiving, present your requests to God. And the peace of God, which transcends all understanding, will guard your hearts and your minds in Christ Jesus.

If you are seeking God's direction in determining the person you should marry, God will show you his answer in a variety of ways, but always with an accompanying peace. This peace is not always a "feel good happiness" (I cried frequently during premarital counseling as we worked through some painful issues), but rather a quiet assurance of a right decision.

Doubt, restlessness, and strife are the opposites of peace. If those are present most of the time in your relationship, it may be an important red flag to heed.

If you are looking over this list of questions with a potential marriage partner in mind, I hope you can answer yes to most of them. If that is the case, you can be confident that together you have the important ingredients for a healthy marriage. If not, you may want to reevaluate your reasons for wanting to marry this person. If you are still dating, keep these guidelines around and use them toward developing your own *ten questions*. They will help you in your dating assessments. Remember that to *find* the right person you must *be* the right person. To find a mate who is spiritually challenging, worthy of respect, sexually pure, and teachable in heart, you need to cultivate those qualities in yourself.

I have you in my heart.

Postscript to ponder: How does your boyfriend match up to these character qualities? How do you match up?

Chapter 17

Dear Lynn:

I saw an object lesson tonight at our team meeting. A little boy named Kade wanted the green balloon, but already had a blue one he was playing with. One of the women, Kendra, was tying a pen to the balloon string so it wouldn't float up to the ceiling, should Kade let it go.

While she had it in her hands, making it more fit for his little hands to hold onto and enjoy, he kept asking for the green balloon. But she very gently looked at him, handed him the blue one, and said, "No, this one is for you."

I felt as if Jesus whispered for me to pay attention to his voice saying, "No, this one is for you," in reference to the life I am living.

The "grass is greener" syndrome is a nasty thing, but it has cropped up in my life this week as yet another former student called to make sure she had my correct address, in order to send me a wedding invitation. (I think that's about the fifteenth in the last three years.) I have started to feel like, "Oh, I want the green balloon;" that is, I want a life more stable, with less pain, with easier decisions, less angst. But a couple of weeks ago on my way home, I heard Jesus whisper, "No, this one is for you."

And do you know what? As Kade took that blue balloon and started playing with it, he totally forgot about the green one.

So, what am I to learn? To live the life God has given me to the fullest, and not to waste time longing for a different one. It was a good object lesson.

Affections of the Heart

> There is nothing but heaven worth setting our hearts upon.—Richard Baxter

Dear Friends:

I found myself enticed by the cover of *People* magazine today. Why am I so enamored by the lives of celebrities? I found myself wanting a kitchen like a friend of mine, with its cherry wood cabinets and slate floor. Why am I so enthralled with material possessions? I found myself wishing for longer legs and a smaller nose. Why do I allow discontentment to deceive my heart? At times, I have found myself longing for a different life. As my friend wrote in her letter, I want the green balloon I cannot have instead of the blue balloon God has given me.

I used to take smug satisfaction in reading the Bible account, found in Exodus 32, of Moses when he came down from the mountain to deliver the Ten Commandments to the Israelites and found them worshipping a golden calf. This grievous event occurred after God had freed them from slavery in Egypt, helped them flee the soldiers by parting the Red Sea, and provided quail and manna for them in the wilderness. Idolatry was how they repaid God for his faithfulness.

"How could they? How dare they, after all God has done for them?" I declared. "I would never worship a golden calf!" Reminding myself of the third commandment, "You shall have no other gods before me," I breathed easy. You won't find me worshipping another god. But Jesus skillfully dismantles my smug superiority in his Sermon on the Mount in Matthew 6, preached on a hillside near Capernaum. There, Jesus told the people what their attitude toward the Law should be, and he challenged the proud and legalistic religious leaders of the day (would that be me?), calling them to *internal obedience* rather than *external observance* of his commandments. Position, authority, and money are not important in God's kingdom,

Jesus told them. What matters is faithful obedience from a sincere heart.

Jesus warned against storing up treasures on earth, the modern-day version of worshipping a golden calf. Such treasures include material or financial wealth; popularity or position; pursuit of the "grass is greener" syndrome—anything we have come to love in a way *that crowds out our love for God.* "For where your treasure is, there your heart will be also," Jesus explains in Matthew 6:21. Instead, he speaks of storing up heavenly treasures: a heart fixed on knowing, loving, and serving God and fulfilling his purposes. Let us guard jealously our relationship to God and let nothing come before it or against it—not celebrity worship, house envy, body image grumblings, career angst, or marital status.

Where are you allowing your heart's affections to rest? Jesus alone is your life. Are you drawing life from any source other than God himself? Ask God to show you where your heart might be *divided* between him and any earthly treasure. Then pray, "Teach me your way, O Lord, and I will walk in your truth; give me an undivided heart, that I may fear your name."[1]

I have you in my heart.

Postscript to ponder: Is any person, material thing, or life goal coming between you and your relationship with God?

Chapter 18

Dear Lynn:

I just took my mom to dinner to celebrate her birthday, which is tomorrow. She said she watches how I live, the pace I keep, and it makes her want to catch her breath. I try to reassure her that I am thirty years younger than she is, and sometimes the way I live makes me want to catch my breath, too. Yet, when I am quiet and take a moment to evaluate how I'm actually living, I think I should be doing more. Perhaps not more activity, but somehow investing more energy toward God's kingdom, like mentoring someone, or praying more, or working at the place that feeds homeless teens—something more than I am doing now.

I haven't been reading Scripture near enough these days. Generally, when I'm tired, I forget that reading Scripture is actually refreshing. One of my resolves this year is to re-implement the discipline of studying Scripture. Aside from wanting to reclaim time spent with Jesus (and reclaim a good walking regimen), I am preparing for an art exhibit. I've got a good deal of work ahead and need to focus.

No man has decided he wants to sweep me off my feet yet. Still single as ever. I'm a little tired of living so much of my life on my own. But for now, it's what I've got to work with. So, here's to solitude, hard work, opportunity to move about freely, and the chance to pursue a dream.

Living With Boundaries

The fruit of righteousness will be peace; the effect of righteousness will be quietness and confidence forever. My people will live in peaceful dwelling places, in secure homes, in undisturbed places of rest.—Isaiah 32:17–18

Dear Friends:

When I was single, Sundays were hard for me. I missed my family who lived a thousand miles away. After church, the afternoon seemed to stretch before me, the reality of Monday hit, and the loneliness set in. I sort of let Sundays happen to me, and when the day ended, I was not brimming with the abundant life Jesus promises. I was lonely, fretful, self-focused, and weary.

A friend of mine, a single in her mid-thirties, has taken a different approach. She has decided to embrace Sundays as her personal day with God. After attending church and lunch with friends, she designates the rest of the afternoon as her "catch up" day and asks for God's guidance in how to spend it, while inviting him to spend it with her. Sometimes my friend needs rest so she will escape to the beach, take a nap, journal, or go for a walk. Other days, she attends to laundry, bill paying, or grocery shopping. If Frisbee golf sounds inviting, she will go; if solitude is calling, she'll stay home. My friend protects her personal day in the face of many opportunities and relationships that clamor for her time. She knows what she needs: intentional time with God and a block in her schedule to be responsible to the tasks he has given her to do. She has set up boundaries.

◆   ◆   ◆

God is a God of boundaries. One of his first acts in the flurry of activity called creation was to set up temporal and spatial boundaries to bring about order from chaos.[1] On the first day of creation, God created day and night; on the second day, the firmament. On day three, he created the seas and dry land. Such fixed boundaries are what make life on this earth possible: God created boundaries for our well-being. In the same pattern as creation, God orders *our lives* through boundaries. Consider these examples:

Each human life span is divided into decades, and each decade presents unique challenges. For me, my 20s began the journey of discovering who I am before God; the 30s taught me how to serve others. The 40s are unfolding as the decade of understanding how to enjoy God. In each decade, God has revealed himself to me in a new way. He has given me roles and responsibilities that have changed over time.

Each year is divided into four seasons, a consistent reminder that our lives are also composed of seasons. This is your season to be single. For most, it will evolve into a season of marriage, then most likely parenthood, and perhaps, later, widowhood. Each season is marked by God's faithful intervention along your path. There will be seasons of personal progress and flurries of creative activity, and seasons of dormancy and waiting. There will be cycles of fruitfulness mingled with barrenness. In each season, we must be willing to declare, "To God be the glory" for his faithfulness.

Each day has twenty-four hours divided into intervals of rest and work. To function well, my body needs to sleep for eight of those hours. It must eat too, and exercise. There must also be time set apart for reflection and solitude, laughter and conversation. We live within boundaries that God intentionally established for our good. It follows that we would do well to establish healthy boundaries in other areas too: emotional, financial, and social.

◆　　　◆　　　◆

Emotional, or heart, boundaries. The Bible's admonition to "guard your heart" is the call to set up emotional boundaries to protect your "wellspring of life." This would include precautions in what you share and with whom; what you let your eyes see, in movies, in print, and online; and where you let your thoughts go, taking every thought captive from the world's diversions and perversions. If you have a boyfriend, you are probably aware of the importance of creating physical boundaries in your relationship, yet emotional boundaries are just as important. Don't whisper "I love you" too soon; don't begin naming your future children with him; and be careful for the right timing to share about your past. In this way, you are setting healthy emotional boundaries as a single woman.

Sometimes friendships require boundaries. Lonely friends will press you for unlimited amounts of your time; you would do well to establish some limits. My friend Kim had a friend who began "dropping by" every evening during dinner. This friendship began to exhaust Kim's generosity and soon she became resentful of this woman. Eventually, Kim spoke up and told her friend to choose one night a week to join her for dinner. Now Kim can plan for that evening and enjoy her company. We need to establish such parameters in order to be fully present to people in our community and be able to offer them strength and support.

◆ ◆ ◆

Financial boundaries. In our "buy it now" culture there is an underlying message: You'll miss out if you don't act quickly. But buying thoughtlessly or without planning can send you over the cliff financially. We are a debt-laden culture; we are being buried alive in credit offers. If you have a problem living within your means, *don't* be ashamed, but *do* seek help from a credit counselor or financial planner.

◆ ◆ ◆

Social boundaries. Most singles I know struggle with being too busy. For the Christian single woman, living within social boundaries is challenging because of a voice inside that whispers, "Do this, do that, don't stop or you'll miss out." I heard that voice many times when I was single, and it deceives some of my friends today.

Another voice in Christian circles is equally destructive because it sounds spiritual. To the mature, ministry-minded woman it whispers, "Since you are single, Serve! Serve! Serve! You have no excuse to say no, unlike married women, and you need to validate your significance through Christian service." This message haunts the single woman in ministry who, though her intentions are good, serves to the point of exhaustion, feels guilty saying no, and depletes the reserves of energy necessary to order her personal life. In doing so much "for God," she misses the restoration that comes from being still and simply enjoying him. As my mentor Harriet muses, "I wonder how much of the stuff we do is just stuff in our schedule—though it may be *good* stuff, even *great* stuff—but not *God's* stuff."

It is sometimes hard to say no to an opportunity when the alternative is to sit at home alone. But solitude has its benefits, and you are never alone when the Father is with you. In *The Imitation of Christ*, Thomas à Kempis writes, "In silence and quietness the devout soul makes progress and learns the hidden mysteries of the Scriptures.... For the further she withdraws from all the tumult of the world, the nearer she draws to her Maker."[2] Jesus always knew when he needed solitude. He would go to a solitary place to pray; step into a boat and drift away from the crowds; or find quiet moments in the early hours of the morning. Whether you are an extrovert or an introvert, carving out time each day for silent reflection and prayer with God will pay huge dividends in your perspective and setting of priorities. During prayer, ask God to show you how he has gifted you and to what purpose he has called you during this season of singleness. Wait on him for guidance before saying yes to service.

◆   ◆   ◆

Conversational boundaries: I am the queen of foot-in-mouth disease. Not long ago, I attended a dinner party and, as the evening waned, I shared an inappropriate story at the table. It was blatant, uncharitable gossip. My husband darted me a "STOP" look, but I continued down the burning bridge of slander. It ruined the tone of the party, and we all quickly disbanded. I was so embarrassed when I got home that I stayed up quite late writing notes of apology to the host and every guest in attendance. It was a humbling experience; how much better it would have been to remain silent. If you struggle with discretion in speech as I do, continue surrendering this area of your life to God's pruning, and he will transform it. Maturity is a great thing when it comes to foot-in-mouth disease.

Another challenging area of speech that requires boundaries is the temptation to share too much with the wrong person. On one hand, transparent and honest sharing can be an encouragement to the body of Christ. Sharing struggles with discretion enables others to enter into community and pray for you. On the other hand, sharing can also be manipulative. I have shared private matters with people to get them to like me, or to make me look spiritual, or to entice men into inappropriate intimacy. I am learning to pray for wisdom as I enter social situations. I try to walk into parties uttering a silent prayer that I would represent Jesus well, that my motives would be pure, and that I would remain silent when appropriate.

◆   ◆   ◆

God gave the Israelites the Law and the Ten Commandments as a framework for living. God established these boundaries in order to strengthen the people's relationship with him and with each other. The Law also was given as a reminder that we can never fulfill God's demands of righteousness in our own strength. When Jesus came, he fulfilled the Law and wrote a new law on our hearts.[3] We are still called to not murder, but now that includes not being angry at each other. We are still called to not commit adultery, but now that includes not lusting after another person. We are still called to not worship other gods, but now that includes refraining from anything that divides our hearts from the Father.

Can we attain such standards by our own efforts of being good? The Apostle Paul says, Not possible! It is God at work in us that makes us act and produce this kind of living. "We are confident of all this because of our great trust in God through Christ. It is not that we think we can do anything of lasting value by ourselves. Our only power and success come from God. He is the one who has enabled us to represent his new covenant."[4]

I grew up attending a church that had this verse engraved on the wall behind the altar: "You are not your own, for you have been bought with a price."[5] As a child, I didn't understand that verse. As an adult, I believe it hints at the idea of holy boundaries. The verse prior says, "Your body is a temple of the Holy Spirit who is in you...." The verse following says, "... therefore, glorify God in your body." In other words, if I have surrendered my life to God, I am no longer the one in charge. I have put boundaries around my desires and given God permission to override my will for his will. My life belongs to Jesus, paid for by his blood; I am merely a steward of it. I surrender all aspects of my life to him: my body, my heart, my finances, my time, my social engagements, and my conversations.

In all these areas, we can live for God's glory or live for our own glory. You are not your own: you were bought with a price. Listen to God's voice and trust his guidance. He will teach you wisdom and the blessings that come from living within boundaries.

I have you in my heart.

Postscript to ponder: Is there any area in your life that needs boundaries in order that God may be glorified?

Chapter 19

Dear Lynn:

I have struggled physically, emotionally, and spiritually for about six months. The endometriosis was the external manifestation of a struggle already deep within. I know that I am dealing with an imbalance of chemicals in my system, which leads to melancholy and depression. Fortunately, I have a doctor who is attuned to my well-being.

The spiritual struggle is something I have yet to put my finger on, but perhaps God will reveal it to me in the future.

The emotional part is tied in with the others, and I find myself lethargic, fatigued, and battling resignation and the desire to withdraw from community.

The verses that keep me going are from Psalm 27:13–14 (NASB): "I would have despaired unless I had believed that I would see the goodness of the Lord in the land of the living. Wait for the Lord. Be strong, and let your heart take courage; Yes, wait for the Lord."

Please pray for me.

Scaling the Depths of Depression

A human being is capable of depression; otherwise, there would be no capacity for exaltation.—Oswald Chambers

When my spirit grows faint within me, it is you who know my way.—Psalm 142:3

Dear Friends:

Depression is one of the most wretched companions on this earthly journey, a bitter remnant of our fallen world. It was recognized even during the Dark Ages. This devastating illness is as real as cancer and heart disease, affects nearly 15 million Americans each year,[1] and is the leading cause of disability between the ages of 15 and 44. Though depression makes you feel alone, you are not: studies in the United States show that one of every four women suffers from depression at some point in her adult life.

Depression is a prolonged state of melancholia and an utter sense of hopelessness. It robs us of joy, deprives us of sleep, and paralyzes our sense of calling. Its symptoms are sadness, lethargy, difficulty sleeping, change in weight, inability to focus or finish things, a racing heart, a sense of being overwhelmed, anxiety, a withdrawing from places and people, a loss of interest in things you used to enjoy, and thoughts of suicide.

Humans are made up of body, mind, and spirit. Depression can take up residence and affect all three of these areas. Its cause may stem from a physiological (chemical), emotional, or spiritual source—or a combination of all three. Many sufferers of depression do not seek treatment, for various reasons. Some feel depression is a result of their own weakness, spiritual failings, or lack of self-discipline. Others understand depression could be a result of sin or past unresolved issues, yet are too ashamed to seek help. If you are struggling with sadness that goes beyond the blues, get help. Talk to a doctor, pastor, or counselor.

Depression has stalked me three times in my adult life, once in college and twice while married, and stayed nearly a year each time. I spent a good portion of the winter months of my first year in college depressed to the point of paralysis. I dropped down to part-time student status and could not get out of bed. Alarmed and helpless, I visited my pastor for a weekend. After listening to me for two days, he told me to return to school, take a hiatus from my classes, and try to accomplish one simple task each day. He challenged me to read a chapter in the Book of Acts every morning.

Acts is an exciting adventure story of the birth and growth of the early church. As I read, it stirred my heart. However, what was most comforting in this task as I carried it out in the following weeks was the consistency of routine. I was feeding my spirit with God's Word and attending to my emotional needs with the completion of a small but important daily task.

The depression lifted after some months. Years later, it became clear that another of my bouts with depression was a result of a chemical imbalance, a hormone depletion. I sought help from my doctor, who prescribed medication that helped immensely.

During another season, depression was of an emotional nature as I dealt with low self-esteem and poor body image. I sought help from a counselor. This time, a spiritual component was also present as I felt God's hand on me calling attention to a particular area of my character. I waited and continued communication with God until he lifted his hand in his time.

Arise and Eat. Depression overcame Elijah after a period of great exertion and spiritual ecstasy. The story in I Kings chapter 18 recounts one of the most wondrous manifestations of God's power and presence in the Old Testament. It was a faith-building experience for Elijah when he went before 450 prophets of the false god Baal, who were worshipping an altar of stone. When Baal did not answer the daylong cries of the prophets, Elijah stepped forward and built an altar to the Lord. For special effect, he surrounded it with a trench and instructed the people to thoroughly drench the altar with water, and then wait and watch. Elijah called upon the Lord to show the people "that you, O Lord, are God." The fire of the Lord fell upon the altar, burning up the sacrifice—the wood, the stones, and the soil—and "licked up the water in the trench." The people fell down and acknowledged God as the one true God.

In the days following Elijah's encounter with the prophets of Baal, he was physically fatigued and emotionally exhausted, depleted in every way. Those symptoms are red flags that depression could follow. When Elijah encountered a different challenge, he seemed to forget God's power in his life. He became terrified of a threat from King Ahab's wife, Jezebel, who said (paraphrased), *"I'm gonna get you."* He sought no display of God's might this time. Elijah ran for his life, sat under a tree, and prayed that he might die. Like Elijah, we are prone to forgetting God and sitting down in despair, even after a spiritually charged season in our lives.

God ministered to Elijah in his depression. As Elijah lay asleep under the broom tree, not caring whether he woke up, an angel touched him and said, "Arise and eat." There by his head was bread and a jug of water. Elijah ate and fell asleep again. The angel came a second time and touched him, saying, "Get up and eat some more, for there is a long journey ahead of you." Elijah did so and was revived.

Whether depression is short-lived or feels like a long journey, the Lord has promised to sustain and provide for you out of his grace. Depression leads one to believe that everyone is distant, even God, but that is a lie. If you belong to Christ, your Heavenly Father is but a breath away through all seasons of life. King David writes, "But as for me, the nearness of God is my good; I have made the Lord God my refuge."[2]

Depression will make you feel that you have fallen into a deep, dark cavern. Don't let yourself stay there. Begin by praying and continue to pray, as it says in James 5:13. Analyze your diet, sleep, and exercise routines. Are you depleted? Sort out if you have wandered from God and might be experiencing the natural results of such wanderings. Repent and come back. Choose small tasks you can accomplish each day, and make it your goal to accomplish them. Maintain contact with a few trusted confidants for support. Seek help from a biblical counselor—one who believes in the power of Scripture, the effectiveness of prayer, and the deceitfulness of sin.

The good news is that depression is not our master; God is. Even while we are battling it, we can be controlled by the Spirit (Romans 8:6), serve others with the strength God supplies (I Peter 4:11), and pray for God's grace and provision to scale depression's walls. As my favorite columnist, Andrée Seu, writes, "The condition is just what is common to man, the prescription is still faith, and the grace for it is inexhaustible."[3]

I have you in my heart.

Postscript to ponder: If you are struggling with depression, is God giving you any insight into what might be the cause, and perhaps the way out, of your depression?

Chapter 20

Dear Lynn:

Do you ever cry out the prayer of the man who brought his son to Jesus, "Lord, I believe! Help my unbelief"? There is such a staunch voice in my heart that says, "Just make do," that I rarely allow myself to dream, rarely take Jesus up on the offer of "accomplishing immeasurably more" than I could ask or imagine. I rarely even allow myself to imagine.

But tonight, as an exercise in hope, I want to imagine. Imagine my heart gripped with compassion for people who don't yet know Jesus. Imagine an intimate connection to Jesus and attentiveness to his voice. Imagine joy in the service to my King. Imagine financial means that would allow me to buy a house; that would allow me to give more generously; that would allow me to take my mom to Italy for her 60th birthday next year. Imagine a career that allows me to not always be scraping by. Imagine confidence, a heart that doesn't carry vengeance or seek retribution. Imagine trust in Jesus that brings peace, and understanding for my neighbor. Imagine a sense of rightly directed ambition. Imagine the ability to receive love when it is extended. May Jesus make these things so.

The learning curve is high these days, and there are millions of lessons to be gleaned.

On Being Mentored

In the terrain of the spiritual life, we need guides.
—Henri Nouwen

Dear Friends:

My interest in spiritual things surfaced in junior high; so did my cantankerous spirit as an adolescent. In response to both, or perhaps out of sheer frustration, my father asked a family friend named Marge to spend time with me weekly in a mentoring relationship.

Marge was a single woman in her early thirties who attended our church. My dad respected her greatly, admired her spiritual maturity, and hoped she could handle a rebellious teen. She could and did. Every Monday night for the next *three years*, Marge picked me up in her orange Corolla and drove me to a nearby restaurant for ice cream and a Bible study. She taught me about life and shared God's heart with me. Mostly, she listened to my pint-sized digressions and self-important conclusions. I referred to her as "the woman who is discipling me." She called herself my *mentor*, defined as a *counselor or coach*. Marge was my first, and one of my most influential, spiritual guides. In high school and college, my pastor, Brian, took over as a spiritual guide. God used him to deeply root my faith, coax me out of my spiritual comfort zones, and whet my appetite for heaven. He is a passionate Bible scholar and poet. To this day, whenever I talk to him, time stands still.

Howard Hendricks once said that you need two types of people in your life—an older mentor and a younger person to mentor. I took this to heart and have tried to find women on both ends of the spectrum to take on these roles in my life.

I encourage you, if you have not already found one, to identify a woman in your life who could be a spiritual guide. This could be a formal mentoring relationship (with a structured Bible study) or an informal relationship. Jesus established a formal mentoring relationship with twelve men, asking them to

"Follow me and become my disciples." The Apostle Paul had an informal mentoring relationship with young Timothy, to whom Paul referred as his "true son in the faith." The son of a Jewish mother and Greek father, Timothy was a respected, teachable man who accompanied Paul on his first missionary journey. He watched, listened, and shared life with Paul.

There is great value in having a mentor. Picture the spiritual terrain of our life as a journey through the dense and confusing jungles of the Amazon rainforest. As I write this, my daughter is visiting this place with a mission team. I have never been to the Amazon rainforest, so if you parachuted me into the middle of it, I would most certainly be lost. A spiritual mentor, who knows the way because she has gone before me while following the Lord, walks with me and takes my hand. While the terrain is no less difficult, the path is clearer because I have someone with greater wisdom walking beside me and sharing her insights. She sees the potential pitfalls in my journey ahead and, as my friend Lindsay says, "offers the hidden helps along the way that my eyes aren't yet trained to see."

Jesus told his disciples to "Learn of me." That is the role of the spiritual guide: to "learn Jesus" to a younger woman. Jesus' disciples lived life with him, spent much of the day with him, traveled, ate, and served with him. And during those moments of living life, Jesus imparted truth to them. I say "imparted" because it encompasses much more than "taught." Mostly, Jesus lived truth out in front of them. He used everyday events, parables, and stories to teach them about his Father. Such is the role of a mentor.

Your mentor should know God and have a heart to teach you about him and help you to know him better. She should be someone you respect as well as enjoy hanging out with, whether running errands, doing laundry, or sharing meals. This is the heartbeat of a mentoring relationship: coming alongside of someone in the journey of life. And while you are looking to this woman for her wisdom, look around to find a spiritually younger sister who can benefit from your wisdom. Seek her out and spend time with her, take her hand and encourage her in her faith walk. I have mentored more than a dozen women over the years, and these relationships have become a rich and fulfilling part of my life. Whether younger or older, single or married, women need each other for courage, inspiration, and perspective.

I have you in my heart.

Postscript to ponder: Identify a woman in your life who might serve as a spiritual guide, and, at the same time, ask God to show you a woman who might benefit from your mentoring.

Chapter 21

Dear Lynn:

For the first time of dancing together, Jamie and I did okay. I had a great time. And I really, really want to take dancing lessons.

There are millions of lessons to be learned from dancing. Truly millions! Particularly about following well. Women aren't supposed to move unless the guy guides them, leads them. It's so hard to follow a lead that's indecisive or tentative in his direction, or who is dancing to a different rhythm than the music. But if his partner tries to fill in the gaps, to make up for, or take over the direction of the dance, he never really learns how to lead.

I observed that the people who were having the most fun and who looked the best on the dance floor together had a number of things going for them, like feeling the rhythm of the music in sync together; a high degree of risk and abandonment that allowed them to experiment without reservation; an ability to laugh and shake it off without embarrassment when the dance flopped; and a high degree of trust. And, lastly, a constant give and take. Plenty of parables.

The Dance of Life

> They shall come and shout for joy on the height of Zion, and they shall be radiant over the bounty of the Lord.... And their life shall be like a watered garden, and they shall never languish again. Then the virgin shall rejoice in the dance ... For I will turn their mourning into joy....—Jeremiah 31:12–13 (NASB)

Dear Friends:

Relationships with men are like a dance. You meet a guy, and sparks fly. You talk and go out. The dance begins, but it is awkward. Who leads? You don't know the music. Your first steps are clumsy; you bump each other, sometimes painfully, and apologize. You step on the other's foot. While others seem to be dancing effortlessly, your dance is hard work. Perhaps you should change partners. Then, for a fleeting moment, you're in step. Together, you glide across the floor as one. Your eyes lock, and you smile. There is no pretense; you are dancing!

In Jeremiah 31, God provides the analogy of a dance as a spiritual picture of restoration, joy, and intimacy he wants with you. For the woman whose life is surrendered to Christ, your journey of faith is often like a dance. You meet the Lord and surrender your heart to him. There is joy and elation. The dance begins. At first, it is awkward. He leads, but you find it difficult to follow. You don't know the Lord's music; you falter in his steps. Distractions pull you away, averting your attention from his lead. Sin trips you, and you stumble. Your Lord waits for you to continue the dance: through repentance, cleansing, and grace, you start the steps again.

Other Christians seem to be dancing effortlessly in their spiritual sojourns; your journey of faith is hard work. Then, for a fleeting moment, you are in step with the living God. You begin to dance to the Spirit's rhythm. You hear his words and whisperings and follow his commands. With your eyes fixed on Christ, your greatest desire is to complete the dance well. You experience more and more of the glorious life—dancing, as Larry Crabb writes, "toward a throne filled by the glory of sheer love."[1]

Dancing according to the Lord's leading is called spiritual maturity. Becoming spiritually mature is a life-long process of experiencing God's grace as you commit to "... put into action God's saving work in your lives, obeying God with deep reverence and fear."[2] Do not grow discouraged in this dance of faith if it seems your spiritual maturity is slow in its progress. Surrender to the Lord's lead, and practice being a follower of Jesus Christ.

We cannot expect to arrive at the place where we've got the Christian life figured out. Sometimes God's work is a mystery, and much of this divine dance remains a mysterious endeavor. God gives us his Word, the church, and the institution of the family to help us unravel the divine mystery as we practice our dance steps of faith in community with others.

Here is my prayer for your dance:

O Lord, teach us the dance of life
As you intend it to be lived.
Teach us to dance with you, to follow your lead.
Instruct us to hear the music of your Spirit's voice,
And the rhythm of your promptings in our hearts.
Give us the will and desire
To move in sync with you,
In daily surrender to the Lord of the Dance.

I have you in my heart.

Postscript to ponder: In what areas are you preventing the Lord from taking leadership in your life?

Chapter 22

"Descending the Mountain"
A Poem by Cindi Snedaker

I went back to the mountain
To that holy place
Where your presence once fell on me—
Sacred ground
Where you revealed to me your glory.
I climbed
Wanting nothing more than to see your face—
Expecting you.

I went to this mountain
This fertile place,
Where, before I could even place my foot,
Your Spirit would sprinkle the ground
Causing it to spring forth life;
Where my soul had been caught up
And I tasted heaven.

I went to the mountain—
And found a foreign land.
This dry, barren land
Where my soul felt parched.
I searched for You and called to You—
Yet, in desperation, found that I could only see me
And there was no glory there.

How did I get there?
Where did I lose sight of You
And run ahead—
So lost in my passionate pursuit?

When did my desire to serve You
Become so about me?

I stood atop that mountain
Naked, empty, and alone,
Paralyzed with confusion,
Uncertain what steps could take me home.
A broken surrender,
A cry for mercy,
Disappointment addressed
Failure confessed.

I turned from that mountain
And began a slow descent—
No longer seeking Your glory,
Feeling only the smallness of my own soul,
Humbled by the arrogance
Of my pursuit for intimacy
For it had become my god.
Who am I that You would choose to show me Your face?

I walked down that mountain
And with each step
I became less and you became more.
No longer did I long for the mountain
For my rightful place was here at its feet,
Face to the earth,
Left with only one thing:
That You are God!

Hands Open, Palms Up

For to me, to live is Christ. Whatever you have learned or received or heard from me, or seen in me—put it into practice. And the God of peace will be with you.—Philippians 1:21a; 4:9

Lord, give me the sacred gift of seeing, the ability to peer beyond the veil and gaze with astonished wonder upon the beauty and mysteries of things holy and eternal.—A. W. Tozer

Dear Friends:

I love the story of the Feeding of the Five Thousand found in the gospels. When a large gathering of people listening to Jesus' teaching began to get hungry, Jesus took compassion on them and told the disciples to have everyone sit down for lunch. The disciples grumbled that Jesus was asking them to buy food for such a large crowd. "This would cost eight months' wages!" they protested.

A little boy in the crowd had a couple of fish and five loaves of bread. He knew, in human terms, this would not be enough to feed a crowd. Perhaps he knew that Jesus was God and could do a God-sized miracle. The child, whose own stomach was probably rumbling with hunger pangs, unclenched his fingers and gave his small lunch over to the Master, and then watched to see what would happen next.

We know the rest of the story. Jesus blessed the paltry meal and had his disciples distribute it to the crowd. When everyone had eaten their fill, the disciples gathered up twelve baskets of leftovers, one for each of the doubting disciples.

Jesus could have fed the multitude in any number of miraculous ways. He could have had manna rain down from heaven, or swarms of fish leap up from the sea. Instead, he chose to bless the faith of a child who released his resources, meager as they were, to the hand of the Almighty God. When the boy opened his hands, palms up, and gave over what he had, Jesus worked a miracle.

If you are interested in having your life transformed from the mundane to the miraculous, release your resources to God, hands open, palms up. Begin each day surrendering your schedule, finances, time, talents, words, thoughts, and energies to his kingdom work. With childlike faith, entrust your Heavenly Father to be a good steward of these things. When you give your resources back to him, meager as they are, expect God-sized displays of his mighty power. You will be filled to the brim with wonder and awe.

One day I was vacuuming my house, listening to Andrew Buckton, a Christian musician from England who attended the same church as my brother. As I was listening and thanking God for Andrew's music ministry, I suddenly had an overwhelming prompting to write a check for $200 and send it to Andrew. I had never done such a thing before. I have never met Andrew and did not know his address. It was such an odd idea that I tried to dismiss it. I kept on vacuuming, but the compulsion grew stronger, and I felt an irresistible pull to perform this irrational act. Finally, I could no longer ignore the feeling. Taking out my checkbook, I wrote a check for $200 along with a note: "Andrew, I felt a strong sense just now that you should have this money to further your music ministry. Thanks for blessing me with your musical talents and your heart for God." I found Andrew's address on the CD jacket, threw some stamps on the envelope, and mailed it across the ocean. I finished my vacuuming in peace and forgot the whole incident.

One month later, I was vacuuming again when the phone rang.

"Lynn? This is Andrew Buckton," a voice began. "I got your number from your brother. I had to call to tell you what has happened in my life." In his eloquent British accent, he told me about his God-sized experience. When he opened my letter and found the money sent to him from a stranger in America, he was amazed. *It was the second letter he had received that week* containing money from a stranger in another country and encouraging him to use the funds to further his music ministry. He knew the timing was not a coincidence. In the weeks and months before receiving my letter, Andrew had been asking God whether he should pursue the recording of a second CD. He needed thousands of dollars (British pounds, that is) and had literally ... none. He was a truly starving artist. Then, in a single week, money came in the mail from different corners of the globe. Was God providing an answer?

Andrew wasn't sure, so he took the letters and checks to church that Sunday and stood in front of the congregation. He shared what had come in the mail and asked them to pray with him about whether this was a sign from God to pursue recording another album. Two people in the congregation stood up immediately and pledged large gifts of money toward recording expenses for a new CD. Andrew was stunned, thanked them, and sat down. After the service, several more people approached Andrew and said they, too, wanted to help finance God's work in a second recording. By the end of the day, *all the necessary funds* were pledged that were required to produce a second album. Andrew was profoundly amazed by this miraculous provision, which began with a few small gifts of around $200.

The story comes full circle back to me by way of a blessing. Andrew made his album and about a year later mailed me a copy. The few songs I listened to in my spare moments were beautiful. Not long after, I was preparing a talk for a single women's retreat. My topic was *Contrasting Shadows* found in Scripture: the shadows of despair in contrast to the shadow of the wings of the Almighty. Since I often play a song at the end of my talks to reinforce truth in a poetic way, I had been listening to several different artists but had found nothing appropriate. The day before I was flying out to the retreat, I listened to Andrew's newest album. One of the tracks I'd not yet heard started playing. The entire song was about contrasting shadows. "Shall we dwell in the valley of the shadow of death?" Andrew sung, "or in the shadow of his Almighty arms?" I am convinced the Lord allowed me to be a part of Andrew's ministry because he knew I would benefit from hearing one of Andrew's songs *more than a year later.* That weekend at the retreat, Andrew's music blessed forty women.

I wish I could say these God-sized stories happen to me all the time. They don't, but I am learning to be attuned to the whisperings of the Spirit and follow through when I receive divine promptings. I am learning to see with "eyes of the heart" the bigger story God is telling. God waits to do something profound with a life that has been surrendered to him, with a heart that has released all its resources to him, hands open, palms up.

We live to advance the kingdom of God. If you are willing, God will give you not only the courage, but also the capability to accomplish his purposes. He will multiply your fish and loaves into a banquet of blessings.

I have you in my heart.

Postscript to ponder: Is there anything in your life to which you are clinging tightly that God may want you to surrender to his kingdom work?

Chapter 23

Dear Lynn:

It has been an interesting week at work—several good days, and several difficult days. I am still wrestling with a decision to stay in my job, or not. For now, God has given me a peace about just continuing to wrestle with him, trusting him to open and close the doors of my life.

In an odd sense, I am very excited about the prospect of doing just that, because I know in the depths of my heart that God has my best in mind. Even the difficulties will be used for good things—namely, his glory. Now the challenge will be to remember that, when the difficult times come. I suppose that is the never-ending battle of this life.

Contrasting Shadows

> Even though I walk through the valley of the shadow of death, I will fear no evil, for you are with me.... Have mercy on me, O God ... for in you my soul takes refuge. I will take refuge in the shadow of your wings until the disaster has passed.—Psalm 23:4; 57:1

> Disturb us, Lord, to dare more boldly, to venture on wider seas where storms will show your mastery.—Sir Francis Drake, 1577

Dear Friends:

One evening, my children were in bed and I was snuggled under my covers reading a book about heaven. I had my candle burning, my glass of lemon water nearby, and peppermint foot lotion embalming my feet. The quiet fall of rain outside made the moment quite, well, heavenly! Suddenly, I heard commotion in the hall, a few bumps, the strange sound of water running, a door shut, and all was quiet again. When I begrudgingly went to check the situation, my heart sank and I cried out, "Aargh!" in a tone of utter frustration.

My five-year-old boy had sleep walked into the hall, mistook the stairwell landing for a toilet, and let loose a cascading flood between the slats of the banister, which hit the white tile floor below in a splattering mess. My instant recall back to earth took me down the stairs to my hands and knees wiping pungent, yellow liquid off nearly pale tile over a splashing span of ten by ten feet. It took me a long while to clean it up, and my attitude throughout the endeavor was none too heavenly.

This story is a picture of my life, and perhaps yours as well. Those of us who are followers of Christ can be walking in the joy of God's presence and experiencing the heavenlies, when, all of a sudden, we find ourselves brutally derailed, thrown down on our hands and knees, grappling with the harsh, stinky realties of life.

I know this well. This has been a hard year for me, a year filled with the deaths of two dear friends, with relational fallout from those I thought were allies, and with misunderstandings from women in my church. I have struggled with personal disappointments, fear and insecurity, chronic back pain, and a severe identity crisis. But I have also experienced more glimpses of eternity this year than in my entire life. I have experienced the closeness of God in a profound and tender way. Depending on my perspective, I have found these difficulties can either crush me or act as a chariot to carry my soul onto the heights.

From my study of Scripture, I have noticed the Bible discusses two kinds of shadows. The first is the shadow of death. This shadow passes over us through physical death, as well as through the consequences of a fallen world. We encounter this shadow whenever we experience a sense of futility, despair, or evil. Or when we see the depth of our own wretchedness, or observe one individual's hurtful treatment of another.

The psalmist, David, knew this shadow well.[1] So did God's man, Job, who *seven times* refers to the shadows in his life.

You may be experiencing shadows in your life. Perhaps you are enduring physical pain, sickness, or depression. You may have been badly hurt by friends, or misunderstood by your church, or you might be experiencing the shadows that come from relational heartache, uncertain futures, broken marriages, new jobs, difficult roommates, new communities, loss of loved ones, challenging schoolwork, or new areas of ministry.

I have spent many early mornings walking around my neighborhood praying for women who feel like they are walking through the valley of the Shadow of Death. However, Psalm 23 does not end there. It goes on to say in verse four, "Even though I walk through the valley of the shadow of death, I will fear no evil, for you are with me; your rod and your staff, they comfort me."

There is another shadow the Bible speaks of much more often: the shadow of the wings of the Almighty. God desires that you seek refuge here.

> He who dwells in the shelter of the Most High will rest in the shadow of the Almighty. I will say of the Lord, 'He is my refuge and my fortress, my God, in whom I trust.'²

The dark shadows of our lives are often the very thing God uses to draw us nearer to himself. Obedience, thanksgiving, perspective, praise and worship—these aspects of faith discussed in previous pages—are the vehicles to help you move from the shadows cast by difficult circumstances into the shadow cast by God's everlasting arms and his magnificent wings that enfold you.

Whether I have laid sick in a hospital bed, or heard about the death of a loved one, or huddled in a living room while a friend is in tears, God has reached down and used such pain to become the chariot that took me into his presence.

On a recent Friday, I spent the morning in prayer, ministering to a friend. Now in her late thirties, my friend is working through the trauma of five years of sexual abuse by a neighbor, starting when she was five. During our two-hour prayer time, she began to release herself into God's healing and restoration. It was encouraging, yet exhausting, and I left with a heavy heart over the grievous burdens many women carry. I went to a restaurant for some soup, sat at a corner table, and felt *beckoned* by the Holy Spirit. That is the only word I can use to describe the sense that I was now being called to meet with God. It is rare that I carry my journal, but I had it with me. I felt compelled to pour out my heart to God in writing, which I did in a long lament covering a full page.

Then I felt the call to be quiet and write only the words I sensed God "speak" back to me. I took what felt like *dictation,* and what emerged was a page of beautiful scriptural truth and encouragement that made me weep, despite the stares of confused waiters and the lukewarm soup before me. In one sentence of my lament, I wrote, "I feel very weary, very aware of the battle, very aware of the enemy's onslaughts on my spirit and on my friends. The shadows seem daunting." Immediately,

I felt the tender Spirit's words flow from my pen: "I know the battle is fierce. Be strong and let your heart take courage. I AM above the shadows."

In my pain that morning, God reached down through his indwelling Holy Spirit and enfolded me in his wings. He revealed biblical truth to me; all that I did at that moment was simply choose to be present before him. That was all I could give him: my choice to cry out and then listen. That was my form of worship. In my life, worship has been the key activity that has moved me from the valley of the shadows of death into the mighty shadow of God's wings. Worship has given me a new perspective. As I have listened to music, read Scripture, journaled, listened for God's voice, or merely been present to him in my weakened state, the things of earth have grown very dim. I find myself embraced by the goodness of God and the hope of eternity.

A song has been extremely meaningful to me in the last few years, a song by Andrew Buckton, whose music has been woven into my life story through the gracious work of the Holy Spirit. You can read about this weaving story in my letter titled, "Hands Open, Palms Up." Enjoy the lyrics of this masterful musician, who shares about contrasting shadows in ways more poetic than I can express.

"*When the Silence*" by Andrew Buckton (www.andrewbuckton.co.uk), ©2001, bluecarpetrecords. All Rights Reserved. Used By Permission.

> When the silence comes tucked away inside my mind,
> I can't hear You or draw near.
> Won't you open up my mind that I may know Your ways,
> That I may find you here.
>
> When the compass spins hiding paths that lead to You,
> I can't find my way back home.
> Show me north again, lead me to Your gates of grace,
> That I may enter in.

It's not enough to hope; our lives were meant to worship You.
Let Your love keep filling me, from Your rushing streams of life.
Let me praise You now, for Your redeeming sacrifice.

When all sides of You are clouded by my doubts and fears,
And my heart has closed its doors,
Won't You come to me, my refuge and my hiding place,
Like the times I've known before.

Let me join in with all the angels singing praise to the Lord our God,
Let me find my home in the shadow of Your glory.

When the shadows come, enfold around my heart,
Won't You blow them all away.
When the winter comes, creeping in to freeze my heart,
Enfold me in Your arms again.

I have you in my heart.

Postscript to ponder: How has God enfolded you in the shadow of his wings?

Chapter 24

Dear Lynn:

God has been at work. This last week has been incredibly painful, physically and spiritually. My neck went out of alignment, and it hasn't been the same since. It has been miserable and makes working really, really hard!

Spiritually, I have been struggling and feeling very alone. The feeling of being unchosen in relationships has left me asking many questions and wondering if the problem doesn't lie within myself. I have had much tension even in friend relationships lately, and it makes me wonder what I am doing wrong! All of this has left me feeling rather exhausted and feeling like I should just give up. But just when I had thrown up my hands in disgust and cried out to God in my despair, he moved in closer and brought with him peace and a feeling that it would be okay.

I kind of feel like I have been bearing the cross lately, though it pales in comparison to THE cross of Calvary which caused the ultimate pain! It has brought me to a new point of understanding the pain of Christ on the cross and how lonely and abandoned he must have felt when the Father turned his back on the Son—anguish!

Things with Brad are as odd and tense as ever. Why do relationships with men have to be so complicated? Anyway, I think God might want me to be single for the rest of my life. I am beginning to think that might not be a bad idea!

Lumpiness of Life

It is not you who shapes God; it is God who shapes you. If then you are the work of God, await the hand of the Artist who does all things in due season. Offer the Potter your heart, soft and tractable, and keep the form in which the Artist fashioned you. Let your clay be moist, lest you grow hardhearted and lose the imprint of the Potter's fingers.—Saint Irenaeus

I'm looking for the face I had before the world was made.—WB Yeats

Dear Friends:

I have a friend who is an artist and sculptor, and so, from time to time, she gets to play with clay. God has taught me some amazing truths through her artistry. A lump of clay never apologizes for being what it is. If it could talk, it would rave not about what it is—shapeless, yet full of potential—but what it is becoming. A lump of clay is surrendering to the work of the potter's hand. Its whole purpose is in its *becoming*.

You are that lump of clay. You need not apologize when your normal lumpiness shows itself in its various imperfections. Instead, let us envision in each other what we are becoming under the gentle, transforming touch of the Master's hand. You are made in the image of God. Because you are his child, you bear his reflected glory. As part of the body of Christ, he is transforming you into that same glorious image, from one degree of glory to the next.

> But we all, with unveiled face beholding as in a mirror the glory of the Lord, are being transformed into the same image from glory to glory, just as from the Lord, the Spirit.[1]

Your life is becoming brighter and more beautiful as Christ permeates it with his lordship and you become like him. Rather than feel shame that your lumpiness surfaces at times and your progress seems slow, rejoice that God is creating a masterpiece—a poem—of your life. He is right on schedule in his transformation process. He is maturing you and making you into a new creature, perfect and complete, lacking nothing.[2]

I like the way Eugene Peterson describes us as *lumps of clay being transformed* in his book, *The Message*, a paraphrase of 2 Corinthians 4:5–9:

> Our Message is not about ourselves; we're proclaiming Jesus Christ, the Master. All we are is messengers, errand runners from Jesus for you. It started when God said, 'Light up the darkness!' and our lives filled up with light as we saw and understood God in the face of Christ, all bright and beautiful. If you only look at *us*, you might well miss the brightness. We carry this precious Message around in the unadorned clay pots of our ordinary lives. That's to prevent anyone from confusing God's incomparable power with us. As it is, there's not much chance of that. You know for yourselves that we're not much to look at. We've been surrounded and battered by troubles, but we're not demoralized; we're not sure what to do, but we know that God knows what to do; we've been spiritually terrorized, but God hasn't left our side; we've been thrown down, but we haven't broken.

In writing that portion of his letter to the Corinthian church, the Apostle Paul saw believers as they *truly were in Christ* and how *they would be* when Christ had finished with them.

This display of power and glory is possible because of grace, not works. God has shown his favor to us—that's what grace is, undeserved favor. Our salvation is based not on the fact that we go to church, or are kind to our neighbors, or give money to charity. Our salvation is based on Christ. And that's where our power comes to live differently in this broken world—it comes from being connected to Christ. It does not matter whether you feel glorious. The truth is, as we stay connected to Christ, we can't help but reflect his glory, regardless of our circumstances or brokenness. It's like sitting next to a campfire on a dark night—as you sit closer to the fire, you can't help but reflect its glow.

My friend, this is your time to shine! If you are a mess, *you are God's mess* and, if you surrender to him, God's glory can radiate from your lumpy life. Let's make a practice of deliberately looking around at one another with new eyes to see each other not for what we are, but for what we are *becoming*; that is, what we will be when he has finished his perfect work in us.

I have you in my heart.

Postscript to ponder: In what ways are you God's mess, and how is he transforming you into a masterpiece?

Chapter 25

Dear Lynn:

My heart is cluttered as I struggle with anxiety and depression. I have had some real physical disorders as a result, and I am feeling broken. I know this is where I need to be before the Lord, but it definitely affects all that I do. Anyway, I'm sure you understand the pant I feel for heaven. I'm tired, but I'm also reminded of God's tender and perfect touch.

Emerging Identity

Remain in me, and I will remain in you. For a branch cannot produce fruit if it is severed from the vine, and you cannot be fruitful unless you remain in me. Yes, I am the vine; you are the branches. Those who remain in me, and I in them, will produce much fruit. For apart from me you can do nothing. —John 15:4–5 (NLT)

Dear Friends:

I recently met the beautiful and gracious Miss Spokane, who will try her hand at Miss Washington and, if she gets that far, the Miss America Beauty pageant. We worked together at a fundraiser for a local charity. Charming and energetic, she was exerting great effort to be gregarious, humorous, and congenial.

She reminded me of myself a long time ago. When I was in high school, I decided that to find acceptance, I would try to become a well-liked girl. I worked hard at bursting through the cliques and offering kindness to both the popular and less-popular kids. During my senior year, my efforts were rewarded by being voted the school's homecoming queen. With elation, I wore my flower tiara, attaching my identity to the notion of popularity.

When I hit the college scene, I immediately realized I would not be able to charm 17,000 undergraduates into accepting me. I would have to alter my strategy. Instead, I chose to try to win the heart of the most charismatic young man in our dorm, a redheaded Irish-Italian. He was electrifying, the pulsating heartbeat of the dorm. Where he was, there was vivacity, and I wanted to be in his presence. I flirted and finally won his heart. He would write tiny notes to me, tape them to pennies, and leave them on my bike seat at various lecture halls around campus. At Christmas, he handed me a pair of beige wool mittens, the first gift he had ever given a girl. I felt exhilarated at my sense of victory. After Christmas, I returned to the dorm to find a note on my pillow. It was from the Irish-Italian, telling me he was not ready to get serious with anyone and was thereby withdrawing all attentions toward me from then on and forever. For the rest of my college days, he spoke *not a single word* to me. I was devastated.

Two years out of college, my heart had recovered, though I vowed I would never put my identity so fully in a man again. I married, had children, and turned to my career to forge an identity. As I began to carve a niche for myself in the features department of our city newspaper, I was handed the responsibility of a weekly column on family life. For five years I wrote the 500-word column with zeal. I was stunned to receive a phone call telling me the section was being restructured, and I would no longer be writing the column. Again, I was devastated. I suffered another identity crisis.

The problem with rooting our identity in anything but the person of Jesus is that every other human endeavor or relationship will eventually disappoint, crumble, or fail. I know this by experience, yet the Bible provides further proof. Does beauty make a firm foundation for identity? Proverbs 31 says, "Beauty is fleeting." How about wealth? Proverbs 23 says, "Do not wear yourself out to get rich.... Cast but a glance at riches and they are gone." Nothing temporal will provide a sure foundation: neither a graduate degree, nor a lavish home, nice car, well-balanced stock portfolio, wealthy husband, clever speech, or well-managed career path. As it says in Ecclesiastes 1:2, 17 (NLT), "Everything is meaningless.... like chasing the wind."

One advantage of your twenties and thirties is beginning to discover the answers to these fundamental questions: Who am I? Where do I fit? What is my calling? The Heavenly Father, who made you with unique talents and gifts, uses this first era of adulthood to begin to unveil the mysteries of you. As you begin to catch glimpses of your God-given strengths, passions, and talents, it is easy to put your identity in the gift, rather than the Giver. In my life, I have tried on various identities—Friend to All, Winner of Men's Hearts, Journalist Extraordinaire, and Perfect Wife, rather than establishing a firm identity as Daughter of the King.

"For in him we live and move and have our being."[1] The Apostle Paul, who spoke these words, correctly established his identity in the changeless, sovereign, unfailing person of God. If you are in these formative years, you would do well to do the same.

It does not mean, however, that we can achieve a godly identity in a single moment. You won't wake up on Monday and say, "Today, I hereby once and for all declare my complete and total identity to be wrapped up in God. I will never again look to people, or career, or material goods to establish who I am or bring me security."

Our spiritual maturity is a process, which is why I titled this letter Emerging Identity. As we spend more time with Jesus, we will begin to resemble him. Then we will discover that we care more about pleasing him than our career accomplishments, personal goals, and material accumulations. We will find ourselves starting to think like Jesus, grieve over what grieves him, and love what he loves. Slowly, over the years of our faith journey, we will begin to understand what Paul meant when he said, "For me, to live is Christ," and what Jesus meant when he said, "I in you and you in me, the vine and the branches."

From what do you derive your identity? Is it from one of the many hats you wear: employee, church worker, comedian, boss, teacher, girlfriend, civic leader, missionary, grad student, board member, community activist, party planner? Or do you desire to proclaim with conviction, "For me, to live is Christ"?

As you begin to ask God to ground your identity in him, he will give you the grace to function in your various roles from the perspective of stewardship and servanthood. If you do a good job, he gets the glory; if you fall short, you are not condemned. You are free. That is the result of proper identity: freedom. You will know your identity is rooted in Christ when you can say, "My career is haphazard, my relationships are confusing, my finances are dwindling, and my future is uncertain, yet it is well with my soul."

"For me, to live is Christ." The journey toward spiritual maturity means that we can say this with more certainty tomorrow than today.

I have you in my heart.

Postscript to ponder: Ask God to show you how you are beginning to resemble Jesus.

Chapter 26

Dear Lynn:

It is just after 8:00 p.m. at Starbucks. I noticed a woman who was sitting alone with a bouquet of roses at a table not far off. She was dressed in pink—almost all in pink—with long, dark hair pulled back in a pink clip, alone with a book and a dark pink drink.

Later, I noticed Pink was still alone, onto a second drink, and reading First Chronicles, but not engaged in it anymore. I invited her to sit with me, to keep company while she waited for whoever it was she was waiting on. I thought to myself at one point, "I have never been a Pink Girl...."[1] as I observed how much pink she had on—even her overcoat was pale pink wool. And here I am wearing my red and black hooded fleece, not proud of how I got snooty in my heart toward Pink, whose Bible was even pink.

She had a story that seemed full of pain, and inklings of hope for a more fulfilling life, hopes that seemed so fragile they might disintegrate if you only looked at them straight on. Along with the Bible, she held a book entitled, *Somebody Loves You*, a message it seemed like she needed to hear.

Perhaps pink is a balm of comfort when you wrap yourself in it, a balm to soothe the ache of being overlooked, and having dreams that have somehow been sabotaged. Perhaps it is a shield of protection against the memories of rejection that have somehow convinced you that even fifteen minutes of company with a stranger in a coffee franchise is precious enough. Any attention that makes you feel less alone is worth celebrating with extravagance, any attention that makes you feel like you belong to someone, somewhere.

Where Do I Belong?

The Road goes ever on and on
Down from the door where it began.
Now far ahead the Road has gone,
And I must follow, if I can,
Pursuing it with eager feet,
Until it joins some larger way.—J. R. R. Tolkien

You belong to Christ, and Christ belongs to God. Think of us as servants of Christ who have been given the work of explaining God's mysterious ways.—1 Corinthians 3:23–4:1 (CEV)

Dear Friends:

My artist friend, Stefani, sees the world around her in piercing, profound colors and contrasts. If someone is sitting in a coffeehouse with fragility written on her face, Stefani sees it. She noticed the heartfelt longing of the woman in pink. At various times, the question in Stefani's heart has been the same: Where do I belong?

I have another friend I'll call Jaime, who has been asking this question for a while. "I feel like I fit in everywhere, but don't belong anywhere," she told me. But lately, Jaime's lack of fulfillment and loneliness seem more acute. She has a greater need to look forward to something on her calendar. She has a stronger-than-ever desire to make her life count, and a sense of wondering what she has to show for the years since high school.

Perhaps you feel the same. You are in a community of friends, but often feel distant from them. What if you stopped showing up—would anyone miss you? Your job seems a misfit; you certainly don't belong there. And church? It seems full of expectations of wholeness, while you feel broken. It is full of married people, and you are single. You're shuffling between singles groups because, well, you are waiting to belong.

I believe God is stirring Jaime's heart—and perhaps yours—in an intentional and profound way in order to answer this vital question: Where do I belong?

The question is critical because we are meant to belong. I love the idea that we were created out of the laughter of the Trinity.[2] God the Father, Jesus the Son, and the Holy Spirit were enjoying each other's company so greatly, they wanted you to be a part of it. We weren't meant to be alone; God put us on this earth to be in community. We were created to belong.

So where do you belong?

After study and prayer on this question, I believe our lives include four areas of belonging.

◆   ◆   ◆

A Grand Story
First, you belong in a story larger than yourself. Perhaps this is a new thought to you, or perhaps you have heard it so often it is dangerously becoming cliché. Don't let it.

As daughters of the King, we are part of a very big thing going on. God is telling a story through his people, and we are part of it. It is a story that started before time and will continue into eternity. It is a story of rebellion, wanderings, heroic rescue, redemption, boundless love, brutal warfare, and a glorious ending. You and I have fallen right in the middle of this story, not by chance but by God's design.

If you are a follower of Jesus Christ, God pursued you and won your heart. Whether it was a month ago or ten years ago, God called you to a friendship with himself through faith in his Son. He pursued you in order that you may love him, glorify him, and enjoy him forever. We cannot forget, however, that we have landed in a story, which means we are real-life *characters* with critical roles. God wants you to live in a story larger than yourself, in a calling he has tailor-made for you. If you will "take the stage," so to speak, and enter into his larger story, I am certain of a few things in your life:

You will feel that you belong.

You will realize your life has significance.

You will understand how everything thus far in your life—the good and the bad—God is using to prepare you for this role. And we desperately need to be prepared, because this story has its share of danger. For some mysterious reason, God has asked us to join his larger story of advancing his kingdom on earth *in the midst of a dangerous war.* The book of Ephesians describes it as a war not between humans, but between God and Satan—a spiritual battle between the forces of good and the forces of evil.

Yet God has ensured that his warriors are well-equipped. He has provided you with spiritual armor.[3] He has created you with unique life experiences (even the painful ones) from which you can draw perspective and wisdom. He has imparted to you spiritual gifts; that is, unique abilities empowered by the Holy Spirit to strengthen God's people.[4] Moreover, you have a measure of faith that God promises to increase if you ask. You are properly prepared to enter into God's larger story, and you are not playing your part alone. Jesus has promised to go before you, walk alongside of you, and never leave you.

So where is this story taking you? I have discovered that this story takes us into a second area of belonging.

◆　　　　◆　　　　◆

The Global Church

You belong in the *church*. Our part in God's larger story is played out through our belonging in the *church*. I don't mean your specific church down the street. I am talking about the church as the global body of believers that needs your unique blend of experiences, talents, and spiritual gifts. You belong to this community—not the building where people congregate on Sunday mornings, but wherever followers of Christ are banded together—and this community vitally needs you to accomplish its mission of calling out to a desperate world, "Jesus is the answer!"

I like how Dallas Willard refers to the collective church as the "called-out" people of God, "empowered to stand up for wandering humanity to see." Willard writes, "When faced with starvation, crime, economic disasters and difficulties, disease, loneliness, alienation, and war, the church should be, because it alone *could* be, the certified authority on how to live to which the world looks for answers."[5]

This mission isn't easy however. You, as part of the body of Christ, are crucial to its success. Wherever there are followers of Christ, there are needs; wherever there are needs, there should be someone ministering to those needs. Some "ministries" are formal, with well-defined goals, tax-exempt status, and letterhead stationery. Others are informal, such as two people praying together, or ten people gathered for Frisbee golf. We need to belong to a community because God calls us to use our spiritual gifts in community to build up the body of Christ to maturity.

George McDonald writes, "Every one of us is something that the other is not, and therefore knows something—it may be without knowing that he knows it—which no one else knows. And, it is everyone's business, as one of the kingdom of light and inheritor in it all, *to give his portion to the rest.*"[6]

Is there a need within your Christian community you've been made aware of, and a way to minister to that need, either formally or informally, to which God is calling you?

◆   ◆   ◆

The Darkened World
While belonging to the church, we also play our part in God's larger story through our belonging in the *world*. The world is the sea of humanity that is still in rebellion against God. It is the culture in which we live, where the Bible admonishes us to "be in but not of."[7]

This means we are to live and work within the world—the full kaleidoscope of seekers, misfits, God-haters, humanists, skeptics, the lonely, lost, and despairing—but not to identify ourselves with the world's priorities and perspectives. Our role among these people, whom God loves, is to be messengers of the gospel, salt, light, shelter, and a city on a hill.[8]

God has placed us in the world not for our own prosperity, comfort, or gratification. We have received God's saving grace in order *to be fitted* to show the world the face of God, through Jesus, who is the light of life. Your nature is being transformed in order to suit you for this task, which means it is not optional or an afterthought. This light we radiate is not what we *do*, but who we *are*. Is there a need within the world that you've been made aware of, and a way to minister to that need, either formally or informally, to which God is calling you?

If you are restlessly grappling with the question of belonging, perhaps God is stirring your heart to ready you to take the stage in a specific role in the church or the world. I have found in my life that when God is readying me for the next stage of my faith journey, he *sparks in me a passion*. On an airplane six years ago, God stirred in me a sense of passion to write this book to encourage single women in their journeys. Other times, he has directed me to counsel women in crisis pregnancies, host a women's retreat at my house, teach an Alpha course, serve dinner to homeless men, mentor college students, teach fifth-grade Sunday school, support Young Life, teach the Bible to new Christians, and so on.

What is God giving you a passion to do? Our passions are often God's way of directing us toward a specific calling that he has prepared for us. The Apostle Paul says it this way in Ephesians 2:10: "For we are God's workmanship, created in Christ Jesus *to do good works*, which God prepared in advance for us to do."

Frederick Buechner has helped me discover my calling by challenging me to identify my "deep gladness." He writes, "The place God calls you to is the place where your deep gladness and the world's deep hunger meet."[9]

If you can identify a "deep gladness" that ministers to a particular segment of the church or the world, the next question to ask of God is: Where specifically are you calling me to serve? God may answer that question through a Bible verse, a conversation with a friend, a vision, a song, a prayer, or an inexplicable conviction. When he provides the direction, the final issue to settle is this:

Will you step onto the stage for which God has prepared and fitted you, and join him in telling his larger story? Or, will you choose to stand off-stage (as we are all tempted to do because of fear or unbelief) and wonder why others seem to lead such compelling, God-infused lives?

You have a role in this story. Your role may or may not include being a wife, but God knows your heart and will perfectly fulfill your need to belong as you surrender to his calling on your life. This calling may include difficult circumstances such as sickness or the death of a loved one. It may mean parenting children as a single mom after enduring an abusive marriage. It may mean a job demotion, a transfer to a new city, or a layoff. On the flip side, your calling may include exciting circumstances: selling your first painting, finishing a marathon, taking a risk to record a CD, or establishing a home for troubled youth. Whatever your role in this life, God promises to do "immeasurably more than all we ask or imagine."[10]

Give yourself the freedom to imagine in a grand way.

Let's say you find a place to serve, in the world or in the church, and you start deriving great joy from it. Joy is a natural byproduct of serving God. Take care that you don't attach your identity to the service, the *doing* of your faith, rather than to Jesus, the *person* of your faith. If you are like me, it is easy to master the ministry: learn it, obsess over it, control it, and ultimately attach a sense of identity to the *calling* rather than to *Christ*. Which leads to the fourth area of belonging. You belong *in Christ*.

◆   ◆   ◆

In Christ
The New Testament mentions the term "in Christ" more than 200 times, and this identity is central to a deep sense of belonging. "In Christ" is a term of *identification*. To be "in Christ" means, "in him we live and move and have our being."[11]

He is your identity, your namesake ("Christian"), your refuge, your credentials, and your cachet—an indication of approval carrying great significance. If you are "in Christ," you have a place to call home. I love the way Brent Curtis describes this idea in *The Sacred Romance*, when he writes:

> When we give up everything else but him, we experience the freedom of knowing that he simply loves us where we are. We begin just to *be*, having our identity anchored in him. Our identity begins to coalesce, not out of doing, but out of living with a good friend for a number of years and simply finding we have become more like him.[12]

Having this place of belonging, in Christ, doesn't mean you will never again be lonely. Even Jesus was lonely. It means you have a purpose, the company of Jesus, and a significant role in his story. You need not feel adrift as a single woman. The next time you are at a party and the familiar wave of "not belonging" crashes over you, consider responding in this way. First, recognize that your adversary, Satan, may be at work to paralyze you with the notion of being a misfit who will never belong and deserves isolation. Satan loves to isolate the follower of Christ. Renounce the temptation toward isolation and *command the enemy to leave at once* by the authority given to you in the name of Jesus Christ. Then, invite Jesus to remind you of why you belong at that party and to Whom you belong. You are specifically at that party with something to offer. God has given you life experiences, unique talents, and spiritual gifts that are vitally important to someone in that room. Moreover, you belong "in Christ," which means you have access to as much confidence, power, wisdom, and perspective as you care to draw upon. You have a role to fulfill, and your part is vital to God's grand story. Since you possess a fragrance of life[13] step out with boldness and make your mark in that room, with the cachet of the living God going before you. Ask God to give you spiritual eyes so you don't miss a thing he has in store for you.

Strike up a conversation, and watch God give you a profound sense of belonging.

If God is stirring your heart to take the stage in the larger story he is telling, this is an exciting time for you, a time to respond in faith and action.

I have you in my heart.

Postscript to ponder: What is the biggest thing you want God to do with you, or for you in these next five or ten years? Then, trust him to do bigger. You belong in his story, playing a vital role in advancing his kingdom.

Chapter 27

Dear Lynn:

The holidays this year caused some turbulence in my heart. The ache to know God more and yet my apparent lack of discipline to further that process has left me frustrated, tired, and somewhat defeated.

The turbulence was not caused by outward circumstances as much as it was by my own inward longings and pain. I have been struggling with fully accepting and knowing God's love for me. It has rattled my faith and left me more vulnerable than I thought possible. Along with [my struggle] come feelings of not being good enough or adequate for God's love. I have to choose daily to trust the truth that I know and to reject the lies Satan feeds me. This is difficult for me to decipher, and I often get lost in the process!

I look with hope to the coming year—I don't want to despair—and, as you have reminded us, we have a God who rules and reigns and gives us eternal hope. I hope God gives me grace to deal with life's struggles, heartaches, and shortcomings. I so desperately want to rest in the ache and embrace it!

The Diamond I Wear Is Within

Diamond is a mineral, a natural crystalline substance, the transparent form of pure carbon. Diamond is indomitable, the hardest surface known. Diamond is exotic, formed in earth's interior and shot to the surface by extraordinary volcanoes. Diamond is superb, the peerless "king of gems" that glitters, dazzles, and symbolizes purity and strength.— Diamond Exhibition, American Museum of Natural History

We are His workmanship, created in Christ Jesus for good works, which God prepared beforehand, that we should walk in them.—Ephesians 2:10 (NASB)

Dear Friends:

This chapter's letter is from a friend who struggles with knowing and accepting God's love, a struggle that is universal to those of us who are fragile humans living in bodies we're unhappy with, thinking thoughts about others we're ashamed of, and seeing ourselves as unworthy of any good thing. If only we truly understood how God sees us as his children.

God gave me a strong calling to write this book in order to provide single women with a heavenly perspective. When the writing of this manuscript was nearing completion, it was time to give the book a title. Since it is a collection of letters to and from single women, I decided early on the title would be *Letters to 20s*. However, over the months I realized that title was too narrow; I wanted this book to encourage single women of all ages and stages, so I changed the title to *Singles Speak from the Heart*. It seemed fine enough, but little did I know God had something else in mind.

Last spring, I attended a woman's retreat and was sitting in the back row of the chapel, listening to the speaker. There was a window cracked open next to me. What happened next felt as if something flew in the window with a message and placed it over my thoughts. The message was articulate and unmistakable: "Your book will be called *The Diamond I Wear Is Within*." I hadn't even been thinking about my book and, suddenly, the Holy Spirit had given it a title. It was such a moment of clarity that I looked around to see if anyone else had seen anything unusual. A smile crept over my face, and I felt like jumping up and down. That title was exactly the message I had hoped to communicate through these pages.

Whether or not you wear a diamond on your finger, if you have been reborn in Christ, you—individually and collectively as the church—are the bride of Christ. Because of this union, you radiate God's glory to a watching world. And it is not because of your own brilliance that you shine: it is a reflected glory, a gift from God by grace. Moreover, in God's eyes you are beautiful. He calls you his workmanship, his masterpiece. Ephesians 2:10 (NASB) says, "For we are His workmanship, created in Christ Jesus for good works, which God prepared beforehand, that we should walk in them."

In order to get a better grasp of the word *workmanship*, a word packed with promise, let me take you to Italy, specifically to Rome where we find St. Peter's Basilica, home of the *Pieta*, Michelangelo's famous sculpture of Mary cradling her crucified son. If it is true that art is a "window into heaven," let us take a moment to consider this great masterpiece in order to catch a glimpse of God's view of you.

Michelangelo was in his early twenties and relatively unknown to the world when he was commissioned in 1498 to do a life-sized sculpture of the Virgin Mary holding Jesus. In less than two years, Michelangelo carved from a single slab of marble the most magnificent sculpture ever created. It was the only one of his works on which he carved his name. In God's eyes, each of us is such a masterpiece. Yet, the *Pieta* does not come close to how God views you as his handcrafted work of art. The *Pieta* was a marble slab; you are created in God's image. The *Pieta* is a lifeless stone; you are a living stone, precious and choice in the sight of God. The *Pieta's* life is temporal and fixed; your life is eternal and in the process of transformation.

If we could forever sear the profound truth of Ephesians 2:10 into our collective hearts and minds, it would profoundly alter the way we view all of life and our role in it, both individually and as the church. The Greek word for workmanship is the word *poiema*, from where our English language has derived the word *poem*. And how fitting, since, in the same way the poem is man's highest literary expression, we are the apex of God's creation, the highest form of his poetical expression. You are God's handcrafted work of art. God designed you deliberately and shaped you distinctively to serve him in a unique way.

You are his workmanship, *poiema*, and he has carved his name on your heart. Whether you feel needy and inadequate; whether you are a misfit and feel displaced; whether you have been sexually abused and feel tainted, the truth is that you are his workmanship. "You are a new creature in Christ; the former things have passed away, behold all things have become new."[1]

We are a collection of flawed women, living out lumpy lives. How could we possibly be God's works of art? It certainly isn't a result of our own efforts. Thanks be to God that we do not have to make ourselves cookie-cutouts of a model Christian woman. Rather, the Bible reveals that our flaws and imperfections are the very things God uses to increase our dependence upon him and thereby increase his glory.

We are his workmanship. When I shared this truth with a friend named Carmen, she could not accept it. Verbally abused by her father for her entire life, this 40-something woman told me, "I just can't believe that for myself." As much as I want to, I cannot convince Carmen of truth, but the Word of God can. Beginning with passages such as Ephesians 1 and Isaiah 43, the Bible is full of evidence that you are his workmanship. The diamond you wear *is* within. God is working out in your life a tremendous demonstration of his glory—glory that encompasses his vast wisdom, lavish love, and resurrection power. Through his Holy Spirit, he is teaching you, training you, bringing you along, sculpting you in exactly the right places to produce a marvelous masterpiece.

We read in 1 Peter 2:9, "You are a chosen people, a royal priesthood, a holy nation, a people belonging to God, that you may declare the praises of him who has called you out of darkness into his wonderful light." God's chief aim is his glory, and we are his chief exhibits. Ephesians 2:10 provides the details of how this is accomplished: it happens through good works. Good works are any deeds that bear fruit and bring glory to God. We are not saved by good works; we are saved *for* good works.[2] Out of a renewed mind, a grateful heart, and a surrendered will, we bear fruit that benefits those around us. The book of First Timothy exhorts us all to be "rich in good works"; that is, to take part in all kinds of general good works like serving the poor and widows, loving each other fervently, practicing hospitality, honoring our parents, and giving generously. Jesus said in Matthew 5:16 (NASB), "Let your light shine before men in such a way that they may see your good works, and glorify your Father who is in heaven." However, in Ephesians 2:10, the Apostle Paul goes further to hint at a glorious mystery. God has prepared a unique set of good works specifically for you. Paul says that God has fitted you for certain good works in advance, when he chose you before the foundation of the world. It was then that God planned for you to take part in a unique set of tasks, callings, and giftedness with the purpose to glorify him through these fruit-bearing works.

This is when the body of Christ becomes compelling. Each of us has a part to play in this larger story as we radiate Christlikeness. Some good works are for a season; others are ongoing. Some good works are public in nature, benefiting many; others are private in nature, benefiting just one. Do you have any idea how many good works God has prepared for you? The situations are there, ready and waiting for you to step into as you walk in faith and dependence upon Christ. This is God's calling for you. As you carry out these good works, you step into the sphere of God's activity and become a vivid display of the greatness and the glory of God. Whether we are twenty-one or ninety-one, this gives our lives tremendous meaning.

What should we do? We should walk in these good works by faith. As always, we have a choice. We can choose to walk according to the good works, which God has prepared in advance for us to do; or we can walk according to our own game plan. But guess which path bears more fruit? It begs the question, "In my life, do I want to bear some fruit or much fruit for God's kingdom?" If we choose to abide in Christ, we will bear much fruit as we walk in the good works God has planned for us, one step at a time,

How do you know what good works you are to do? Get to know yourself. God has shaped you for specific good works through your abilities, interests, talents, spiritual gifts, personality, and life experiences. With all these factors in play, God will prompt you toward a good work by giving you a passion for something, or by placing a burden on your heart, which compels you to take action. If we take time to listen to the whisperings of the Spirit, we will come to recognize God's promptings. The next time you read Scripture, hear a sermon, or watch the news, pay attention to the stories that stir your heart. God often stirs our hearts to prepare us for one of his promptings. We need to be spiritually attuned, and, over time, we will come to recognize the voice of God. Then, it only requires a willing heart to say yes, and step out in faith and do the next thing.

I am not saying to go and create work for yourself. Our lives are already too busy. I think the key is to free up our schedules and create a little margin, so that when the Holy Spirit prompts you to do a good work, you are able to say yes. It might mean saying yes to making a phone call or writing a letter of encouragement, even when it is inconvenient. It could mean saying yes to serving a roommate or family member, even when you are tired. It might mean saying yes to a volunteer opportunity, which could require saying no to another. Or, saying yes to changing jobs, moving, breaking up, or giving away your money. Doing good works is usually not easy or convenient. It takes a decision of the will, apart from how we feel.

Jesus is our best example of walking in good works. The secret to Jesus' life was that he exemplified a heavenly perspective. I am challenged to do the same. When life doesn't turn out as we planned—whether we have wayward children, we're single when we want to be married, we have career confusion, we're struggling financially—instead of asking "why me?" this verse challenges us to cultivate a different perspective: "I believe, Lord, that I am your workmanship. As your masterpiece, Lord, where are you taking me as you write the poem of my life?"

I have you in my heart.

Postscript to ponder: Dwell on the biblical promises below, and then step out in faith according to whatever good works God is calling you to do.
  You are beautiful and loved by God.
  Your life has value.
  You have been given a specific calling for your days.
  God is moving your life toward the fulfillment of his calling for you.
  You have gifts and a place in the church.
  God understands you and knows you.
  God is making new your inner person.
  God is in the process of maturing you.
  God is changing your name.
  God knows the number of your days; you are not forgotten.
  God is not withholding any good thing from you.

Chapter 28

Dear Lynn:

I am always trying to prove myself to others and myself. I give power to the voices of the world and put myself in bondage because the world is filled with "ifs." The world says, "Yes, I love you if you are good-looking, intelligent, and wealthy. I love you if you have a good education, a good job, and good connections. I love you if you produce much, sell much, and buy much." There are endless "ifs" hidden in the world's love. These "ifs" enslave me, since it is impossible to respond adequately to all of them. The world's love is, and always will be, conditional.

Battling Cynicism in a Cynical World

Our truest heart longs to worship.—Jan Meyers, *The Allure of Hope*

In my distress I called to the Lord; I cried to my God for help. From his temple he heard my voice; my cry came before him ... He mounted the cherubim and flew; he soared on the wings of the wind ... He rescued me because he delighted in me.—Psalm 18:6, 10a, 19b

Dear Friends:

I almost missed the wave dancers. We were driving south on California's coastal highway on a recent vacation when suddenly, out of the corner of my eye, I saw colors flitting on the ocean below the cliff. We quickly exited Highway 1 and parked close to the bluff overlooking the beach. I jumped out of the car, ran toward the ocean, and saw a wondrous sight: wetsuit-clad men and women on small sailboards holding on to enormous kites of bright colors. There were five in all, but our eyes were fixed on the red kite surfer. He was speeding over the surface of the water heading toward the beach, effortlessly flying over the surf, and then instantly swiveling around on the board and skimming back out toward the vast ocean. As he hit a wave head on, he would pull up on the kite and soar into the air for twenty or thirty feet, float above the white, frothy water, spin while airborne, and land gracefully while continuing at rocket speed along the water's surface. He was wave dancing, never minding the ominous surf hurtling toward him that could crush him in an instant. As I watched him, I was caught up in the beauty, awe, and exhilaration of this single moment. Man and creation seemed to be painting a majestic picture of God's wonder, and I was a witness to it, a great mystery that caused my soul to soar.

Those moments of exuberance are rare for me. Mostly, I battle being caught up in a life where disappointments, misunderstandings, fatigue, and monotony threaten to pummel my perspective. My husband and I have been hurt by fellow Christians. We've watched friends of ours choose to cheat on their spouses. We have been financially swindled by individuals we trusted. These stabs of betrayal entice us to choose the way of cynicism. We live in a cynical world, and it is a challenge to keep from succumbing to it.

The word *cynical* means "contemptuously distrustful of human nature and motives." A cynic is one who is pessimistic, fault-finding, ill-natured, and critical; one who believes people act solely out of self-interest. Cynicism often takes the verbal form of sarcasm; its close cousins are resentment and resignation. Cynicism is a protective mechanism we construct to deal with pain, disappointment, and fear. It is a hard shell that we think will protect us from the world's brokenness. Unfortunately, it is also a hard shell that keeps us from experiencing the wave-dancing wonders of God. Cynicism is the opposite of biblical love that "bears all things, believes all things, hopes all things, and endures all things."[1]

Therefore, if God is love, cynicism cannot be of God. That is the lesson I am learning lately, as I march onward through middle age to eventually face that fork in the road that older people must face—the junction where they must choose the path of becoming either "bitter," or "better." If left to my own tendencies, I am at risk of becoming bitter, but God is showing me a better way.

In my studies of Christ's character, I can resolutely declare that Jesus possessed not a speck of cynicism. He got angry but never cynical. He understood the sin of the world but was not contemptuous toward sinners. He was a man of sorrows, but not a man of cynicism. He sat on a hill above Jerusalem and wept in grief for a people who were in rebellion, but he never stopped showing the kind of love that keeps bearing, believing, hoping, and enduring. As followers of Christ, it seems we have two choices as we face life's disappointments. We can walk the path that embraces cynicism, or walk the path that embraces

Christ. If we want to become women who live along the second path, what can we do to get there and stay there?

To answer that question, the Lord has given me a single word upon which to meditate: *glory*. This small word symbolizes mysteries so profound and other-worldly that great scholars have for centuries grappled with its meaning. To begin to understand glory is like peeking through the crack of a door into another dimension. We get a glimpse of something Beyond. We glimpse splendor, illumination, and immeasurable joy through the sliver of an opening, but we can only glimpse it partially. The Apostle Paul alludes to this mystery in 1 Corinthians 13:12 (NASB) when he writes, "Now we see in a mirror dimly, but then face to face; now I know in part, but then I shall know fully...."

Even a glimpse of God's glory is a remedy against cynicism. The word glory encompasses greatness, honor, radiance, splendor, and majesty. In Hebrew, the word refers to *a visible manifestation of God*. In Greek, it signifies "the fullness of who God is and what he does, as exhibited in whatever way he reveals himself, particularly in the person of Christ."[2] Glory is a word we cannot fully grasp because it represents the King of Glory who cannot be contained in human terms.

The Bible mentions the word glory nearly 300 times. In the book of Exodus, in the story of Moses and the Israelites, glory is mentioned fourteen times. If ever there was a man who had a good cause to embrace cynicism, Moses was that man. God had just freed the Israelites from slavery in Egypt, parted the Red Sea so they could escape the Egyptian soldiers, and performed numerous miracles to provide them food and water in the desert. In Exodus 32, Moses returned from a mountaintop moment with God and saw the people of Israel dancing around a gold calf, a large idol they had erected because they had given up on God. Moses' anger burned "... and he threw the tablets out of his hands, breaking them to pieces at the foot of the mountain. And he took the calf they had made and burned it in the fire; then he ground it to powder, scattered it on the water, and made the Israelites drink it."

Moses had the choice to seize cynicism but, instead, he chose to embrace God in the midst of his distress. He returned to the Lord, repented on behalf of his people's sin, implored God for forgiveness, and asked to receive a glimpse of God's glory. On the verge of diving into despair, Moses asked God, "Now show me your glory!"[3] God consented to pass by Moses and give him a glimpse of his glory. Later, when Moses carried two new stone tablets in his hands up Mount Sinai, the Lord came down in the cloud and stood there with Moses, proclaiming his name, the LORD. The effect was so profound Moses bowed to the ground, worshiped, and prayed. Yet, it was not the prayer of a proud man who had placed himself above the golden calf worshippers. Instead, Moses uttered a prayer of contrition: "Although this is a stiff-necked people, forgive *our* wickedness and *our* sin, and take us as your inheritance."

I am challenged by Moses' example to embrace God in the face of disappointment, rather than delve into cynicism. I am learning to take my laments to the Lord and ask for his forgiveness for any part of my brokenness for which I am responsible. God's glory changed Moses' perspective, ushered him into his presence, and left Moses with lingering hope. I am learning from Moses to present myself to God and ask him boldly, Show me your glory! It is God's desire that his children seek his presence. He wants to be found. He wants to be known. He has chosen to leave the tabernacle of the Old Testament and dwell among his people, in our hearts.

I am learning from Moses to respond to life's disappointments in worship and let hope restore me, rather than let cynicism destroy me. Hope is the firm conviction that not all will remain as it is. Hope is the confident expectation that God is ultimately in charge and will not disappoint. C. S. Lewis writes in *The Weight of Glory*, "The cross may come before the crown and tomorrow is a Monday morning, but there will be a crown!" When we choose to worship—in the car, at work, doing laundry, or writing bills—heaven becomes accessible to melt away cynicism. One cannot be cynical before the awesome and wondrous King of Glory.

If you are in your twenties, you are entering the season of life where disappointments will come steadily and surely. If you are beyond twenties, you already know this to be true. Your friends will let you down, as will your employer, church, and family. You have a choice to grow in bitterness or grow as a woman who seeks and finds God. If you make a habit of choosing the first path, cynicism, it will gain a foothold and grind you into a bitter woman. If you choose the second path, God will make himself known to you, his presence will go with you, and you will find comfort even amidst your disappointments. Your heart will be restored, and you will abound in hope and love. As you become a reflection of God's glory, cynicism will flee, and wave-dancing wonders will abound.

I have you in my heart.

Postscript to ponder: How has God shown you his glory amidst life's disappointments? What are some tangible ways you can embrace the hope of Christ, rather than the futility of cynicism?

Chapter 29

Dear Lynn:

When someone tells their story, usually they are aware of the audience but, in this case, I have no idea who is listening, and therefore I have the freedom to delve deep into my soul, risk-free.

After graduating from high school, I decided to go to San Jose State. Well, I really didn't decide to go there, I actually wanted to go to Long Beach State, but we had limited funds. One of my mom's boyfriends was a millionaire and invited me to live with him so I could attend SJSU. That plan folded two weeks before school started when the millionaire backed out of his deal. It took several weeks to get me into the dorms, but when I finally got in and was able to live on my own, the freedom became too much. My pursuit of drugs, sex, and alcohol became a daily struggle for me. My first semester of college became a whirlwind of drunken frat parties, obtaining a few boyfriends, using illicit drugs, and showing up sporadically to class. I was wasting my mother's second mortgage money, and I was feeling the pressure of it.

Not only was I playing the alcohol and drug scene, I was also trying out for the softball team. Believing I was good enough, I banked my college career on playing and on receiving a scholarship. Boy, was I wrong. After being cut in the second round of tryouts, my dream ended. The only reason I went to college was to play sports, and now I had nothing. I had no family life to go back to, and I wasn't great academically, so college was out of the question. I drowned my sorrows in alcohol, drugs, and men, thinking there wasn't much to live for in life.

In both high school and college, I made several attempts on my life and once tried to bring it to completion. Sitting there in my dorm room, sobbing my eyes out, I was getting up enough guts to make one slice in my wrist, and all I could do was carve a simple little cross in my hand. That little pain of carving the cross, with a piece of sharp glass, held my inner pain for one more day. That night and the week to come became the worst seven days of partying I had ever done. I must have passed out about three of the nights, recovered during the day only to throw up for the other four. I was frying my body to death, but I didn't care since I didn't have a life I wanted to live.

On November 30, seven days later, I received a phone call in the middle of the day, from a group on campus. They never stated who they were, but explained to me that I'd filled out a survey on campus and marked the box to "call me." I listened to their talk and at first denied their invitation to meet, but then remembered it was dry week at SJSU, due to finals study week. I figured I would be able to meet new people to party with since I was too young to buy beer at the local 7-11. I met with them the next day. To my surprise, they weren't the party group I was expecting. They introduced themselves as Campus Crusade for Christ, and I went ballistic. I must have called them every choice word in the book. They deceived me by not telling me on the phone they were a religious group on campus. I quickly walked away from them, but they followed just as quickly. I heard the pitter patter of feet behind me and whipped around yelling at them with a few more choice words. They apologized and asked if they could talk; I, of course, declined. One of them, before I could escape, said to me, "You look like you're athletic, what do you play?" I turned around and said, "I play softball, basketball, and volleyball." She hooked me in with, "I played volleyball at UC Santa Barbara."

We stood there talking about sports and life for fifteen minutes until they asked to go sit down. We proceeded to sit in the middle of the student union, and surrounding me were the men from the fraternity where I was pledging to be a little sister. You could say I was a little nervous being with these religious freaks. After all, I had a reputation at stake. I was the life of the party by night and wishing I was dead by day. We sat down, and one of the women asked if I had ten more minutes; I said "of course," as I thought we would talk more about college sports. Boy was I mistaken, as Marianne pulled a huge Bible out of her backpack and put it on the table. I freaked and asked her to put it away as others would see the book on the same table I was sitting at. She did and then asked if she could read this tiny orange booklet called, *The Four Spiritual Laws*. I carefully scanned the people around me, making sure no one was looking as I hunched over the table and quietly replied, "yes."

I sat in a hunched position as she opened the book and went over the "Laws." I was amazed at what I was hearing. God loved me and offered a wonderful plan for my life. I thought, "Yeah right. No one loves me." Before I could put my thoughts around Law 1, Law 2 was, "God died on the cross for your sins." No way could anyone die for all the mistakes I have done in my life and *who in their right mind would?* I started becoming the devil's advocate and asked them outrageous questions. They were patient and continued in their reading.

We came to some circles in the book. One was a circle of a crazy life with a cross on the outside and the other was an organized, perfect circle with a cross in the middle. They asked me which one I was. Of course, I was the crazy, discombobulated circle. They then asked which one I would like to be. They must have thought I was stupid as I thought for so long, but I answered the question with my gut: "The organized circle." They were surprised!

Something was happening inside me as each Law was spoken and each verse read. I was becoming anxious, soft, and emotional. My guard was down; I was allowing someone to get to me. I was allowing myself to feel. I haven't felt these feelings since I was a young kid. They scared me to death, but I continued.

They came to Law 3, which explained that if I accepted Christ into my heart, he would live with me and forgive me of my sins. No way! No one person could do that, but I sat there *wanting it so much*. I wanted someone to love me, to live with me, and forgive me. I was changing inside, and I was frightened. I almost ran away from the table, but something or Someone kept me there.

They came to the fourth and final Law: the sinner's prayer of repentance. They read it as they were supposed to, and closed the book. I sat up quickly and yelled, "What are you doing!" With a frightened look, one of the girls said in a stutter, "I thought you wouldn't want to accept Christ." I excitedly said, "I do!" She then frantically searched for the right page. She couldn't find it. This book was only around ten pages; how could you not find it? The other older woman, Marianne, put her hand on the girl's hand as she strummed through the pages and opened the book to the prayer. She asked how

I wanted to do this. I had no idea. She explained to me I could pray quietly to myself, pray with her, or keep my eyes open and read the prayer along with her. I chose to read with her.

I accepted Christ that Tuesday in December at 2:15 in the afternoon. Most people say that nothing physically happens to you when you accept Christ, but that day, that *minute,* I felt a huge burden lifted from my shoulders. It was as though I took off a huge backpack filled with bricks. I knew at that point that I was free from my life of sin, guilt, and shame. I am to this day, seventeen years later, still working side by side with God to reprogram my life.

The Stories of Our Lives

Our stories are given to us by God; they are never meant to impact only us.—Jan Meyers

Dear Friends:

I met Christina, the one whose story you just read, about six years ago. She encouraged me to write this book, and her life continues to impact mine.

One Friday night, after spending the evening hearing Christiana's story, I went to sleep thinking about her and God's faithfulness in her life. In the middle of the night, I was suddenly awakened from a deep sleep, and God spoke so clearly in my heart that I felt his words had been audible. "Tell Christina I love her with an Everlasting Love." I had never heard God speak to me in this way, and I was amazed. I delivered God's personal message to Christina the next morning. Our hearts and our stories have been intertwined ever since.

What is the story of your life? We should all be asking each other, "Tell me your story."

Your story, sometimes called your *testimony*, is a record of God's movements in your life and your responses throughout your life. It can be a chronological account or an anecdotal account. Your story touches on the milestones of your life—births, deaths, accomplishments, illnesses, major changes, stresses, heavy heartaches, great joys, brushes with the unseen realm—and how they have shaped you into the woman you are.

One of my dearest friends, Mary Kay, is a master storyteller. She is articulate and well-read; she is a beautiful writer and poet. She remembers details and weaves them into a tapestry of story that delights, encourages, and often brings me to tears. She has penned several important milestones in my life.

My friend Brian also loves stories. When he is getting to know someone he has just met, he prods: "Tell me your story." He says it with a twinkle in his eye and a posture that says, "*Tell it fully, I have the time,"* and then leans in, anticipating the possibility of discovering another piece of the puzzle in the great epic story God is telling through his children.

If you have never given thought to your story, here are some questions to consider:

- ◆ What was my childhood like? How did it shape me?
- ◆ What was my adolescence like? How did it shape me?
- ◆ When and how did God first make his presence known to me?
- ◆ When and how did I respond to God's invitation of salvation?
- ◆ What milestones (good and bad) in my life have shaped me?
- ◆ What has been the biggest lesson I have learned in the past year?
- ◆ What has God taught me about himself recently?
- ◆ What do I hope this year will look like?

The beginning of your story, or even its middle, does not necessarily determine its ending. Jesus' story seemed to be ending in an agonizing way. In an olive grove, the Savior experienced so much grief he spilled droplets of blood as he asked his Father, Is there another way? But his story was not yet over; there was a profound postscript. After his death on a cross, his resurrection happened three days later, followed by his ascension into heaven.

One friend's story involves nine months of a drinking binge and sleeping with any man who would have her. Then God stepped in—through a song on her car stereo—calling that prodigal daughter back to himself. It is an amazing account of God's tender rescue. Her story enlarged my heart for God and my appreciation for his grace and mercy toward us.

"Our stories, the stories of others, and the way our stories collide can add up to increased desire and increased hope if we let them," writes Jan Meyers in her book, *The Allure of Hope*.[1] I certainly need increased hope in my life, and it is my desire that my own story, peppered throughout the pages of this book, will increase your hope and provide an eternal perspective. Because ultimately, our stories are meant to point to *his* story.

As we mature as followers of Jesus, we are joining God's ministry to a dying world, and our stories meld with his story. His is a story of life and death, rebellion and battles, heroic love and redemption. It is a story that started before time and will play out into eternity.

The purpose of sharing your story—a story most likely filled with triumph, pain, and restoration—is to build up the body of Christ and point us to the hope of the Great Storyteller who weaves my story with your story, and who has a profound ending in mind.

Referring to C. S. Lewis' *The Horse and His Boy*, Meyers writes, "Aslan's call to Shasta is the same call Jesus breathes in our hearts: 'Let Me reveal your story to you, and then let Me show you how it fits into Mine.'"[2]

Those are, in essence, Jesus' words to us when he said, "Let not your heart be troubled; believe in God, believe also in Me. In My Father's house are many dwelling places; if it were not so, I would have told you; for I go to prepare a place for you ... that where I am, there you may be also."[3]

I have you in my heart.

Postscript to ponder: What is your story, and how might your story fit into God's?

Chapter 30

Dear Lynn:

"Trust in him at all times, O people; pour out your hearts to him, for God is our refuge" (Psalm 62:8). My heart has been stirred in the past couple of weeks by Erik. Do you know him? I won't go into all of the details, but I have found myself filled with expectation only to be left in disappointment. I read Psalm 62:8, and my heart knows in a new way the incredible blessing that comes from pouring out your heart before the Lord. It is interesting that the psalmist tells us first to trust him at all times, then pour out your heart, then recognize that he is a refuge. It is almost as if we can't pour out our hearts until we are able to trust. That is the result of trust: giving our hearts away. When I trust someone, I am able to let all that is in my heart fall before him. In this act of pouring out my heart, I discover what is true about that person; either they are a safe place and my trust grows deeper, or they wound my vulnerable heart and cause me to retreat. I am learning this to be the truth of this verse.

So all of that to say, the deep passions and longings of my heart to experience God through marriage continue to rise to the surface of my heart. I continue to find myself in a place of having to consciously choose to trust God and pour out my heart to him. Somehow, in the midst of all of this, I am trying to discern what it means to be a friend to Erik, to love him as a brother, to serve him without allowing my heart to become attached prematurely and develop expectations. What is encouraging to me is that the pain of disappointment has not caused me to retreat from him or give up. I desire to walk that fine line of being a friend while not demanding anything from him. Oh, will the struggle of singleness ever be gone? Sometimes I wonder if this is the thorn that God has chosen to leave in my side until he calls me home. I hope he returns soon!

Embracing Singleness Amidst the Stings of Life

The Lord longs to be your husband, your champion, the One who fights for you.—Anonymous

A single person investing heart and soul in the lives of friends, whether married or single, is a symphony. She lives from a posture of admitting her deep thirst for companionship and marriage. There are occasional minor chords because she can look at her life and know that singleness was not God's original intent. These minor chords are mingled with grand major chords, perfectly timed crescendos, and rests, all coming from the ebb and flow of God's work in her life.—Jan Meyers

Dear Friends:

Society has thankfully removed the stigma of singleness. More women are staying single longer and getting married later. In fact, there is wisdom in postponing marriage until you are certain it is God's best for you. Unfortunately, being single still stings at times. How I wish I could wave a magic wand and remove the pain, the longing, and the restlessness from a single woman's heart. When my leg stings, I apply a cooling balm and instantly find relief. Why is that not true in life? Where is God when our hearts sting? What is the balm we can apply?

The cooling balm of relief is biblical truth—the truth of God's goodness toward you, his lavish love for you, the hope he offers, his redemptive plan for your life, and the fact that he is not withholding any good thing from you.

He understands your desires, is aware of your loneliness, created your longings, and is more familiar with your heart than anyone on earth. He is very near to you and offers *gifts* for you to embrace during this season of singleness. To understand the gifts he offers, let me take you to a tiny book in the Old Testament called Habakkuk, the account of a faithful prophet during a season in Judah's history when the people felt uncertain about their future. Perhaps there is a balm for you here.

The story takes place around 626 BC. Known for their violence, the Babylonians had regained their own throne from the Assyrians and were preparing to destroy Judah and Jerusalem as they had done to Judah's neighbors. At the start of the book, Habakkuk carries on a one-way conversation with God, crying out that he is confused. "How long, O Lord, must I call for help, but you do not listen?" From Habakkuk's perspective, things were not as they should be for God's chosen people. God seemed to be tolerating a situation that was clearly wrong in Habakkuk's eyes. Evil seemed to be reigning. God seemed to be silent. Habakkuk wonders aloud, How long must I wait for you? Then God spoke and gave Habakkuk some news, but it wasn't the news Habakkuk was looking for, and was, in fact, quite disturbing. Here is my paraphrase of 1:5–11:

"You are not going to believe this, but things are about to *look* like they are getting even worse," the Lord replies. "In the world's eyes—and maybe in your eyes—my rescue is not going to look like a rescue at all, because I'm not going to remove you from your circumstance right now. In fact, it may even look like I'm failing you and breaking my covenant with you."

Not wanting to lose his spiritual bearings under the weight of such fearful news, Habakkuk's response is to restate what he knows about God[1], as if to remind himself of who God is: "O Lord, are you not from everlasting?"

Habakkuk is still restless regarding God's sovereignty—even challenging God with further lament, essentially saying: "I'm not at all happy with this answer! How can you do this?"—yet reaffirms his trust in the Holy One who is almighty. Then he stands watch, waiting for God's response.

God responds a second time to Habakkuk, this time instructing him to take notes so that others may learn of God's ways. In a lengthy answer, God essentially tells his prophet, "I have a plan and it is good plan. I am going to use this season of uncertainty and suffering to draw you nearer to me. Live by faith. I will reveal my plans for your life at an appointed time. It may seem like I am lingering with that revelation, but wait for it. It will certainly come and will not delay. My ways are eternal."

At first, Habakkuk nearly faints in anxiety upon hearing those words; yet, as the Lord expands on his promise of justice and rescue, Habakkuk comes to the place where he can state that even if all is lost, "Yet I will exult in the LORD, I will rejoice in the God of my salvation" (3:18, NASB). These are not the words of resignation; this is the declarative statement of one who has determined to exceedingly leap for joy because he knows the Lord is trustworthy.

There is much we can glean from Habakkuk's account. His was a dogged climb up the mountain toward accepting God's sovereign plan over what appeared to be injustice in his life. Habakkuk's laments are authentic. So is his waiting. When he doesn't like God's answer, he humbly reopens the conversation with the Almighty. He waits again. Desiring integrity, Habakkuk reaffirms and restates the truth of who God is. He waits again and listens. When God's word comes to him—a clear call to remain faithful—Habakkuk responds in obedience.

Bible scholar David Dorsey suggests that the purpose of the book is to take the audience from a place of "confusion and despair to clarification and hope."[2]

This ascent to the summit culminates in Habakkuk's humble response of worship. "The final chapter," writes Brian Morgan, "contains a psalm of praise, petition, and submission to God."[3] Habakkuk realizes that this time of uncertainty should not blind him to God's salvation or cause him to lose the joy of the love relationship God is offering. The prophet resolves to rejoice in the Lord, even when there is no *apparent* fruit in the circumstance, even when the *symbols of success and prosperity* are removed. Listen in to the final words of Habakkuk's prayer:

> Though the fig tree does not bud and there are no grapes on the vines, though the olive crop fails and the fields produce no food ... yet I will rejoice in the Lord, I will be joyful in God my Savior. The Sovereign

Lord is my strength; he makes my feet like the feet of a deer, he enables me to go on the heights.[4]

One of the themes of Habakkuk is waiting. We can relate. You and I are waiting. We are all waiting for something. Yet, while you wait, the Lord longs to lead you to the heights—his higher place of intimacy where you *can see better*.

When a deer goes to the highest mountaintop, what are the benefits? I see three benefits that await a deer on a mountaintop. These are the same three gifts the Lord is offering you as you wait on the heights: *perspective, provision, and protection*.

◆   ◆   ◆

The first gift, when we follow God to the heights, is divine perspective. The deer on the heights has a greater view of potential food, suitable shelter, and approaching enemies. Habakkuk's perspective is renewed when he accepts that God alone decides how things will unfold, and, in the end, God's people must realign their understanding to his.[5]

It will be easier for you to get through yet another friend's lingerie shower, baby shower, or wedding if you cultivate an eternal perspective, which includes these truths:

- ◆ The Lord is in control and won't mess up his plan for you, which, by the way, is utterly amazing.
- ◆ If his plan for you includes marriage, you won't miss out on finding the right person just because you are at home eating salty snacks and watching reruns.
- ◆ Marriage is not the Promised Land: intimacy with the Lord is the Promised Land, which is available to you right now.
- ◆ Joy, contentment, and rest come not from a human relationship, a white picket fence, or a nursing baby. They come from choosing to obey, and know, and enjoy God who loves you.

- God's goodness for you flows from his love for you. He will not withhold from you anything that he deems *good*.
- He allows storms in your life in order to show his mastery. Don't try to run from the storms; look for his mastery in the middle of them.
- You are not alone; you have a companion that knows you intimately and accepts you fully, delighting in your every breath.

◆   ◆   ◆

The second gift, when we follow God to the heights, is that we begin to recognize God's provision. A deer on the heights can more easily recognize all that is available for life because she is above the shadows, the trees, and the *lions*. God allowed Habakkuk to dialogue with him until the prophet came to realize that God's provision, though seemingly delayed, would come at the appointed time.

You can face a new day as a single woman when you recall all the abundance God has provided in your life. In addition to food, shelter, clothing, friends, and some amount of money, the Lord has bountifully provided you a host of spiritual blessings found in Ephesians 1:3–14. Read those blessings, meditate on them, and celebrate God's provision.

Eve's problem in the Garden of Eden was focusing on what she *couldn't* have, rather than luxuriating in what she *did* have. We should learn from her. My friend Bernard once said, "Don't allow questions you can't understand to detract you from the glorious certainties you already know. God works in a mysterious way, his wonders to perform."

We are called to live in hope, faith, and trust of God's provision.

◆   ◆   ◆

The third gift, when we follow God to the heights, is that we understand our need for God's protection. A deer on the heights can detect dangers more clearly. From its perch of safety, the deer knows where the enemies are lurking and can stand guard. "God revealed to Habakkuk," writes Morgan, "that although persecution and suffering would come and even though it would seem like a long time before justice was done, that the righteous person would trust in God's faithful loyal love to work out the future."[6]

We need protection as we face persecution. We have an enemy who has a stated purpose, "To steal and kill and destroy."[7] In my life, the devil's schemes seem mainly focused on stealing my joy, killing my heart, and destroying my hope. Fortunately, God has equipped us with the armor necessary to fight against such strategies of the devil.[8]

What dangers are lurking about your heart to be on guard against? Here are some you may be battling:

- ◆ cynicism
- ◆ fear
- ◆ shame
- ◆ resignation
- ◆ despair
- ◆ worry

The closer you move to the almighty God, the greater protection he offers against anything that might steal, kill, or destroy.

Perspective, provision, and protection are gifts the Lord offers a single woman in times of uncertainty. These gifts are yours for the taking, but first you need to follow the Sovereign Lord to the heights, which means spending time with him and choosing to be in his presence. In those moments of stillness, you will discover the mysteries of your Maker. You will find that adventure, abundance, and wholeness await you.

> Come, let us go up to the mountain of the Lord. He will teach us his ways, so that we may walk in his paths.
> —Micah 4:2

Will you, like Habakkuk, climb the mountain from uncertainty to faith? Let us not shrink back, but instead be willing to wait in praise, petition, and submission to God. Faith in the sovereign goodness of Almighty God is well-placed faith.

I have you in my heart.

Postscript to ponder: Do you believe God is for you and that he is not withholding any good thing from you? Is there anything that is preventing you from embracing this season of singleness?

About the Author

On an airplane heading home in April 2001, Lynn Gibson sensed a clear calling to encourage single women by compiling a collection of "letters" on a variety of topics from a biblical perspective. These devotional writings would be in direct response to letters she has received in the past years from more than two dozen women. This book is the culmination of that calling.

Lynn has shepherded single women for nearly two decades. Her ministry, which includes mentoring, conference speaking, and Bible teaching, is to encourage, equip, refresh, and remind single women of biblical truth.

Born and raised in Los Altos, California, Lynn earned a B.S. degree from the University of California, Davis. She has worked as a freelance journalist and film critic for the last sixteen years, writing for newspapers, magazines, and online web sites. This is her first book.

Lynn moved to Spokane, Washington, in 1993, where she lives with her husband, Jeff, and their three children. She enjoys gardening, speed-walking, and music. You may write her at: lynn@diamondwithin.org. For more information or to book her for a speaking engagement, please visit: www.diamondwithin.org.

Notes

Introduction

1. 2005 Census, U.S. Census Bureau.
2. Ibid.
3. Alexandra Robbins and Abby Wilner, *Quarterlife Crisis: The Unique Challenges of Life in Your Twenties* (New York: Tarcher/Putnam, 2001), 6.
4. John 14:6.
5. Thank you to the Apostle Peter for articulating my calling in 2 Peter 1:12–13.

Chapter 1—When God Passes By

1. Exodus 33:22.
2. Psalm 34:8.
3. Hebrews 1:3.
4. John 17:24, NLT, italics mine.
5. Lamentations 3:25.

Chapter 2—Finding Christ, Following Christ

1. I like how Oswald Chambers defines sin.
2. John 3:16 and 1 John 1:9.
3. Thank you to my friend and pastor, John Hanneman, who first acquainted me with the term *community*, and demonstrates with his 20s group what it means to live in community.

Chapter 3—Waiting for the Lord (While Tending a Broken Heart)

1 Psalm 42:3, 9.
2 Thank you to my friend and pastor, Brian Morgan, who first illuminated this truth to me.
3 Psalm 42:7–8.
4 Psalm 84:11.

Chapter 4—The Joy of the Wayfarer

1 John 15:5, 10–11, NASB, italics mine.
2 John 16:22, NASB.
3 James 1:2–4.
4 2 Corinthians 4:17–18.
5 Oswald Chambers, *My Utmost for His Highest* (New York: Dodd, Mead, 1935), November 11.

Chapter 5—Seeing the Unseen

1 Romans 8:28, NASB.

Chapter 7—Guard Your Heart

1 Ephesians 3:17.
2 Ephesians 4:26–27.

Chapter 8—Unveiled and Alluring: Some Thoughts on Biblical, Feminine Beauty

1 Genesis 12:11.
2 Genesis 24:63.
3 I Peter 3:3–4, NASB.
4 Galatians 5:22–23.

Chapter 9—Quenching Your Thirst at the River of Life

1. John 4:13–14, NASB.
2. Jeremiah 2:11b, 13, NLT.
3. Jeremiah 2:25.
4. John Eldredge, *The Journey of Desire* (Nashville: Thomas Nelson, Inc., 2000), 137.
5. Micah 4:2.
6. Revelation 22:17.

Chapter 10—I Will Change Your Name

1. Song of Songs 6:3.
2. In Ephesians 1, for starters.

Chapter 11—You're Invited

1. Psalm 40:1–3.
2. Revelation 3:20, NASB.

Chapter 12—Sexual Temptation and the Question of Same-sex Love

1. Don't miss this beautiful story in John 8.
2. John 14:15, NLT.
3. 1 John 2:4, NLT.
4. Romans 1:18–27, NASB.
5. Ephesians 6 outlines our spiritual battle, and the armor of God to fight this battle.
6. 1 Corinthians 6:18–20, NLT.
7. Romans 6:23.

Chapter 13—Eight Words to Change Your Life

1. I Samuel 3:19.
2. Psalm 86:11.
3. Romans 1:21.

Chapter 14—Spiritual Slump

1. Joshua 1:5.
2. 2 Corinthians 4:18.
3. Hebrews 4:15–16, NLT.

Chapter 15—Longing for Intimacy

1. Matthew 23:37.
2. 2 Corinthians 2:16, NLT.
3. Chambers, *My Utmost for His Highest*, January 7.

Chapter 16—Ten Questions Before Saying "I Do"

1. 2 Corinthians 6:14.
2. Hebrews 10:24.
3. 1 Thessalonians 4:3.

Chapter 17—Affections of the Heart

1. Psalm 86:11.

Chapter 18—Living With Boundaries

1. Thank you to my pastor and friend, Brian Morgan, who first shared this concept with me.
2. Thomas à Kempis, *The Imitation of Christ* (London: Penguin Books, 1952), p. 51.
3. Jeremiah 31:31–34, one of my favorite passages.

4   2 Corinthians 3:5–6, NLT.
5   1 Corinthians 6:19b, 20, NASB.

Chapter 19—Scaling the Depths of Depression

1   According to the National Institutes of Mental Health.
2   Psalm 73:28, NASB.
3   Andrée Seu, *"Out of the Blue,"* World Magazine, April 16, 2005.

Chapter 21—The Dance of Life

1   Larry Crabb, *The Pressure's Off* (Colorado Springs: WaterBrook Press, 2002), 104.
2   Philippians 2:12, NLT.

Chapter 23—Contrasting Shadows

1   Check out Psalm 23.
2   Psalm 91:1–2.

Chapter 24—Lumpiness of Life

1   2 Corinthians 3:18, NASB.
2   James 1:4.

Chapter 25—Emerging Identity

1   Acts 17:28.

Chapter 26—Where Do I Belong?

1   This phrase, "Pink Girl," is from the poem, "A Woman of Crimson" by G. Faith Little, first printed in *The Self That Was Her Story: An Anthology of Women's Writings,* ed. Rene´ Marie, (4U2C Printing, 2003).

2. I first heard this idea from John Eldredge and Brent Curtis, *The Sacred Romance* (Nashville: Thomas Nelson, Inc., 1997).
3. For details, check out Ephesians 6.
4. For details, check out First Corinthians 12.
5. Dallas Willard, *Hearing God* (Downers Grove: InterVarsity Press, 1999), 146.
6. George McDonald, *Unknown Sermons* (London: Longmans, Green, and Co., 1885), italics mine.
7. John 17:16.
8. Matthew 5:14.
9. Frederick Buechner, *Secrets in the Dark: A Life in Sermons* (San Francisco: HarperSanFrancisco, 2006).
10. Ephesians 3:20.
11. Acts 17:28.
12. John Eldredge and Brent Curtis, *The Sacred Romance*, 167.
13. 2 Corinthians 2:14–16.

Chapter 27—The Diamond I Wear Is Within

1. 2 Corinthians 5:17, NASB.
2. Thanks to my friend and pastor, Bernard Bell, for his insights.

Chapter 28—Battling Cynicism in a Cynical World

1. 1 Corinthians 13:7, NASB.
2. W. E. Vine, *An Expository Dictionary of New Testament Words* (Nashville: Thomas Nelson, Inc., 1952).
3. Exodus 33:18.

Chapter 29—The Stories of Our Lives

1. Jan Meyers, *The Allure of Hope* (Colorado Springs: NavPress, 2001), 113.

2   Ibid., 167.
3   John 14:1–3, NASB.

Chapter 30—Embracing Singleness Amidst the Stings of Life

1   Brian Morgan, unpublished class notes OT III, Western Seminary, Winter 2005, 5.
2   David Dorsey, *The Literary Structure of the Old Testament, A Commentary on Genesis–Malachi* (Grand Rapids: Baker, 1999), 309.
3   Morgan, *Western Seminary notes*, 5.
4   Habakkuk 3:17–19.
5   Morgan, *Western Seminary notes*, 6.
6   Ibid.
7   John 10:10.
8   See Ephesians 6.

978-0-595-42539-6
0-595-42539-9